Think iFruity

Think iFruity

**A FoxTrot Collection
by Bill Amend**

**Andrews McMeel
Publishing**

Kansas City

Visit *FoxTrot* on the World Wide Web at www.foxtrot.com

YOU BOUGHT A CELL PHONE??

I WAS TIRED OF BEING THE ONLY GUY AT WORK WITHOUT ONE.

EVERY TIME I'D SIT DOWN AT A BIG MEETING, OUT THEY'D COME — THE LITTLE STARTACS... THE LITTLE SONYS... FRED WITH HIS LITTLE Q PHONE...

WELL, I CAN'T WAIT TO SEE THE LOOK ON THEIR FACES WHEN I TRUMP THEM ALL WITH **THIS** BAD BOY!

WANT ME TO GIVE YOU A PREVIEW?

BIGGER IS BETTER, RIGHT?

ROGER, I HOPE YOU DIDN'T PAY A LOT OF MONEY FOR THIS THING.

NO — THAT'S THE BEST PART!

SOME OF THE CELL PHONES THEY HAD COST HUNDREDS OF DOLLARS. SOME WERE AS CHEAP AS A DOLLAR APIECE. BUT YOUR BARGAIN-HUNTER HUSBAND FOUND **THIS** HIDING IN THE BACK!

YOU'RE NOT GOING TO BELIEVE THIS, BUT THEY ACTUALLY **PAID** ME TO TAKE IT OFF THEIR HANDS!

GEE. FANCY THAT.

THE MOBYCOM-2000 (OOF) I ASSUME THE "MOBY" IS SHORT FOR "MOBILE."

ANDY, I CAN'T BELIEVE YOU DON'T LIKE IT!

I MEAN, LOOK AT THIS BROCHURE! LOOK AT WHAT IT SAYS!

"THE MOBYCOM-2000 IS WITHOUT QUESTION THE CADILLAC OF CELL PHONES."

MOBYCOM 2000

ROGER, THEY'RE TALKING ABOUT ITS WEIGHT.

READ THE PART ABOUT ITS SOLID STEEL CONSTRUCTION.

BONK! BONK!

SO HOW DO YOU CHARGE THE BATTERIES IN THIS THING?

ACTUALLY, IT DOESN'T HAVE BATTERIES.

HUH? APPARENTLY, THEY COULDN'T HOLD A CHARGE LONG ENOUGH, SO THE MOBYCOM-2000 USES A DIRECT CONNECTION TO HOUSEHOLD CURRENT.

YOU BOUGHT A MOBILE PHONE THAT HAS TO BE PLUGGED IN?!

THE SALESMAN MADE A GOOD POINT— WALL OUTLETS ARE PRACTICALLY EVERYWHERE.

WHAT ABOUT ON THE HIGHWAY?! WHAT ABOUT IN AN EMERGENCY?!

SEE THESE 10 BUILT-IN CIGARETTE LIGHTER ADAPTERS?

HI, ANDY, IT'S ME. I'M OUT BACK ON THE MOBYCOM.

ROGER, SPEAK UP. I CAN'T HEAR YOU.

I SAID I'M OUT BACK ON THE MOBYCOM!

I STILL CAN'T HEAR YOU.

MUCH BETTER.

HONEY, YOU'LL HAVE TO SPEAK UP.

ANDY, I CAN'T TAKE THIS CELL PHONE BACK!

WHY NOT?!

I SIGNED A LONG-TERM CONTRACT. THAT'S HOW I GOT SUCH A GOOD DEAL.

CAN'T YOU AT LEAST TRADE IT IN FOR SOMETHING SMALLER?

LOOK, I PROMISE THE MINUTE MY MOBYCOM AGREEMENT EXPIRES, I'LL SWITCH TO ONE OF THOSE LITTLE FLIP-TOP JOBBIES.

YOU KNOW, THE KIND CAPTAIN KIRK USES.

"STAR TREK" TAKES PLACE IN THE 23RD CENTURY, ROGER. WHAT ARE YOU SAYING, ROGER?

FoxTrot
by Bill Amend

7

I CAN'T BELIEVE YOU BROUGHT A BAG LUNCH TODAY, PETER!

WHY?

THE CAFETERIA HAS STEAK ON THE MENU!

PAIGE, OUR CAFETERIA DOESN'T SERVE THINGS LIKE STEAK.

IT'S PRINTED RIGHT HERE! IT'S IN BLACK AND WHITE!

AND IN ALL CAPITAL LETTERS, YOU'LL NOTICE.

I CAN'T IMAGINE WHY THAT WOULD MAKE A DIFFERENCE.

AND HOW WOULD YOU LIKE YOUR SQUID TENTACLES, EGGPLANT AND KETCHUP COOKED?

I'VE GOT TO READ THIS WHOLE BOOK BY NEXT WEDNESDAY.

SO? I'VE GOT TO READ THIS WHOLE BOOK BY NEXT TUESDAY.

HA! I'VE GOT TO READ THIS WHOLE BOOK BY NEXT MONDAY!

OOPS. I GUESS IF I HOLD IT SIDEWAYS LIKE THAT, IT'S TOO THIN TO SEE.

WOULD THAT WORK IF I TURNED YOU SIDEWAYS?

...OR UPSIDE DOWN, OR INSIDE OUT?...

MMM. I LIKE THIS.

WHAT?

THIS COFFEE. IT'S DIFFERENT SOMEHOW. DID YOU BUY ONE OF THOSE ONES WITH A FLAVOR ADDED?

NO...

ODD. I COULD SWEAR IT'S GOT SOMETHING IN IT. HAZELNUT... CINNAMON... MAYBE A HINT OF VANILLA...

OH, WAIT. NEVER MIND.

NEVER MIND WHAT?

ANYONE SEEN THE GIANT CRICKET I CAUGHT FOR SCIENCE CLASS?

WOULD WIDDLE QUINCY LIKE A TUMMY RUB?

WOULD WIDDLE QUINCY LIKE A KISSY POO?

WOULD WIDDLE QUINCY—...

BONK! BONK!

JASON, DO YOU HAVE ANY IDEA HOW ANNOYING THAT IS TO LISTEN TO?!?

AN INKLING, PERHAPS.

Paige_is_ugly

INCORRECT PASSWORD. PLEASE RE-ENTER.

Paige_is_a_dolt

INCORRECT PASSWORD. PLEASE RE-ENTER.

Paige_is_a_raving_lunatic_psycho

INCORRECT PASSWORD. PLEASE RE-ENTER.

YOU TAKE LONGER TO LOG ON THAN ANYONE I KNOW.

All_of_the_above

(Beep) WELCOME, JASON FOX.

RRGGH!

OOF!

I DID IT!

WIMP.

JASON, WILL YOU AND THAT GLOBE GET OUT OF HERE?!

FoxTrot
by Bill Amend

RUMBLE.

CUE THE SUBWOOFERS.

WITHOUT WARNING, THE EARTH'S CENTER OF GRAVITY SHIFTS TO SOMEWHERE IN NORTH AMERICA.

THE SPINNING PLANET BEGINS WOBBLING WILDLY LIKE AN OFF-CENTER TOP.

CITIES CRUMBLE! OCEANS FLOOD CONTINENTS! CIVILIZATION, AS WE KNOW IT, CEASES TO BE!

FINALLY, TO ADD INSULT TO INJURY, THE EARTH BREAKS UNDER THE STRESS AND SMASHES INTO THE MOON.

WHAT COULD POSSIBLY HAVE CAUSED THIS?? WHAT COULD POSSIBLY TIP THE BALANCE OF A 6,588,000,000,000,000,000,000-TON PLANET??

PETER, HONESTLY. THAT'S YOUR 38TH HELPING OF TURKEY.

AND I'M JUST GETTING STARTED.

AND PEOPLE THOUGHT INDEPENDENCE DAY WAS FODDER FOR A MOVIE.

MOM, IS IT OK IF I GO OVER TO DENISE'S HOUSE FOR THANKSGIVING DINNER THIS YEAR?

PETER!

THANKSGIVING IS A TIME TO SPEND WITH FAMILY! PRETTY SOON YOU KIDS'LL BE GROWN AND WE WON'T ALWAYS HAVE THESE OPPORTUNITIES TO BE TOGETHER!

I CAN'T BELIEVE YOU'D WANT TO HAVE DINNER AT YOUR GIRLFRIEND'S HOUSE INSTEAD OF HERE WITH US!

WHO SAID "INSTEAD"? OUR DINNER'S AT 2:00; THEIRS IS AT 4:00.

TWO THANKSGIVING MEALS?! ARE YOU INSANE?!

HIGH FIVE, SON.

HI, DENISE. AM I EARLY? LATE?

WELL, LET'S SEE...

MOM'S BUSY IN THE KITCHEN AND DAD'S GLUED TO SOME FOOTBALL GAME ON TV.

I'D SAY YOU GOT HERE AT THE PERFECT TIME.

I MEANT FOR DINNER.

GOSH, WE HAVEN'T SMOOCHED SINCE, WHAT, YESTERDAY?

(I HOPE YOU'RE HUNGRY, PETER. MOM'S BEEN COOKING LIKE A MADWOMAN.)

(WHEN SHE FOUND OUT YOU WERE COMING FOR THANKSGIVING DINNER, SHE WENT INTO SOME SORT OF OVERDRIVE.)

(I THINK SHE HAS A SECRET DREAM OF FATTENING YOU UP.)

(THAT'S OK — I COULD USE A LITTLE WEIGHT.)

YOU'VE BEEN WARNED.

I FORGET... SHOULD I PASS THINGS TO THE LEFT OR THE RIGHT?

THOSE ARE ALL FOR YOU, DEAR.

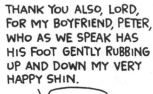

FoxTrot
by Bill Amend

THERE'S SOME MOVIE STARTING IN THEATER 6 IN TWO MINUTES.

THERE'S SOME MOVIE STARTING IN THEATER 14 IN FIVE MINUTES.

THERE'S SOME MOVIE STARTING IN THEATER 9 RIGHT NOW.

TWENTY-TWO SCREENINGS OF THE "STAR WARS: EPISODE I" TRAILER IN AN HOUR. (WHEW) TALK ABOUT A WORKOUT.

AND YOUR MOM SAID IT WASN'T HEALTHY.

CHECK THIS OUT — MY FREE THROWS ARE BETTER THAN THE PROS' THIS YEAR.

MY HOOK SHOTS ARE BETTER THAN THE PROS' THIS YEAR.

MY JUMP SHOTS ARE BETTER THAN THE PROS' THIS YEAR.

NIMBUS, THE PROS ARE IN A LOCKOUT.

WHOA! I MADE ONE! DID YOU SEE THAT?! DID YOU SEE THAT?!

YOU WANTED TO SEE ME?

PETER, THAT WAS MRS. HUMBARGER ON THE PHONE.

SHE SAID SHE SAW YOU DRIVING OUR STATION WAGON DOWN HER STREET TODAY LIKE A RUNAWAY MISSILE.

NO WAY! IMPOSSIBLE! I SWEAR TO YOU, MOM, SHE COULDN'T HAVE!

WE WERE GOING MUCH TOO FAST TO BE SEEN.

YOU KEEP QUIET!

THE KEYS, PETER.

FoxTrot
by Bill Amend

I CAN'T BELIEVE I HAVE TO WATCH "A CHRISTMAS CAROL" ON TV FOR SCHOOL **TONIGHT** OF ALL LOUSY NIGHTS!

WHAT'S WRONG WITH TONIGHT?

MOM'S MAKING HER GARLIC, GREEN PEPPER AND TOFU CHILI FOR DINNER.

AH. THE MEAL OF A THOUSAND NIGHTMARES.

I SHUDDER TO THINK WHAT KIND OF WEIRD DREAMS I'LL BE HAVING.

SO HOW DO YOU LIKE THIS NEW OPERATING SYSTEM?

BAH. DUMB BUGS.

JASONEZER SCROOGE... IT IS I, YOUR FORMER PARTNER...

JACOB MARCUSLY?! BUT... BUT... YOU'RE DEAD!

THAT'S RIGHT, JASONEZER. I HAVE RETURNED AS A GHOST TO TELL YOU SOMETHING.

WHAT?

THAT IF YOU CONTINUE ON YOUR PRESENT COURSE, YOU'LL END UP LIKE ME.

COOL.

I THOUGHT YOU'D LIKE THAT.

OH, MAN, MY SISTER IS GOING TO FREAK!

WHAT ARE ALL THOSE CORDS WRAPPED AROUND YOU?

THESE, JASONEZER, ARE THE CABLES OF THE MANY VIDEO GAME CONTROLLERS I SELFISHLY CLUNG TO IN LIFE.

LITTLE BY LITTLE, I BUILT THESE BINDS, AND NOW I MUST LIVE WITH THEM THROUGHOUT ETERNITY.

I HAVE COME HERE TONIGHT TO WARN YOU, JASONEZER.

TO BE MORE GENEROUS WITH MY TOYS?

TO NOT WASTE MONEY ON THIS ONE BRAND OF JOYSTICK. THE FIRE BUTTON IS SLUGGISH.

HEY, WHY'S THAT LADY SCAVENGING THROUGH MY COMPUTER EQUIPMENT?!

LEAVE THAT ALONE, DO YOU HEAR ME?! THAT COST ME AN ARM AND A LEG!

VIDEO CARD... OBSOLETE. HARD DRIVE... OBSOLETE. CD-ROM, MODEM, CPU... OBSOLETE.

DICKENS WASN'T KIDDING. THIS FUTURE STUFF **IS** PAINFUL.

HMM. MAYBE THOSE TATTERED CURTAINS ARE WORTH SOMETHING.

COOL. A CEMETERY.

WHAT ARE YOU POINTING AT? YOU WANT ME TO LOOK AT THIS TOMBSTONE?

NO, SPIRIT! NOOOO! THIS CAN'T BE MY FATE! SAY IT CAN BE ALTERED! SAY IT CAN BE CHANGED!

JASONEZER SCROOGE
BORN
DIED MAY 20

MAY 20TH IS THE DAY BEFORE THE NEW "STAR WARS" MOVIE OPENS!

YOU THERE! WHAT DAY IS IT?

TODAY? WHY, IT'S A SCHOOL DAY, MR. JASONEZER, SIR!

A SCHOOL DAY! A **SCHOOL** DAY! THE SPIRITS HAVE WORKED THEIR MAGIC IN TIME TO RETURN ME ON A SCHOOL DAY!

DID YOU HEAR ME?!

I'M AS LIGHT AS A FEATHER! I'M AS GIDDY AS A—

I SAID IT'S A SCHOOL DAY, JASON!

ALL RIGHT! ALL RIGHT! I'M UP!

AND YOU'RE ONLY **ALMOST** AS LIGHT AS A FEATHER.

20

FoxTrot

by Bill Amend

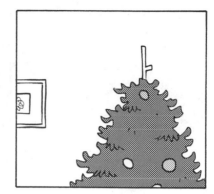

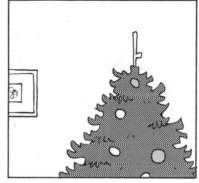

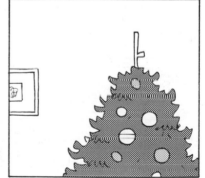

FoxTrot
by Bill Amend

HEY!

I CAUGHT ONE! I CAUGHT ONE! LOOK EVERYBODY— I FINALLY CAUGHT ONE!

WELL, IT **WAS** THERE.

UH-HUH.

WHAT'S THIS?

I'M MAKING A SNOW SCULPTURE NATIVITY SCENE IN HONOR OF THE HOLIDAY SEASON.

THESE ARE THE WISE MEN... THESE ARE THE SHEPHERDS...

AND IN THIS CRIB IS THE TINY SAVIOR OF CHRISTMAS.

HOW CUTE. A BABY CREDIT CARD.

ARE THOSE LIGHTNING CLOUDS FORMING UP THERE?

HO HO!

HO HO! HO HO!

HO HO! HO HO! HO HO! HO HO! HO HO! HO HO! HO HO! HO HO!

JASON, I TOLD YOU — NOT UNTIL AFTER DINNER.

TWINKIE, THEN?

"'TWAS THE NIGHT BEFORE CHRISTMAS, WHEN ALL THROUGH THE HOUSE..."

"NOT A CREATURE WAS STIRRING, NOT EVEN A MOUSE."

PITTER PATTER
PITTER PATTER
PITTER PATTER

YET ANOTHER BOOK WRITTEN BY SOMEONE WHO SURELY NEVER HAD KIDS.

JASON, WILL YOU QUIT TRYING TO SNEAK DOWNSTAIRS?!

THANKS, MOM AND DAD!

THANKS, MOM AND DAD!

THANKS, MOM AND DAD!

FOR THE GIFTS, OR FOR GETTING UP AT THIS HOUR?

CAN YOU TELL ME IF I REMEMBERED TO PUT COFFEE IN THIS CUP?

CARE FOR SOME HOT CHOCOLATE WITH YOUR MARSHMALLOWS?

HOLD ON. LET ME MAKE SOME ROOM.

FoxTrot
by Bill Amend

26

FoxTrot
by Bill Amend

I SWEAR, THIS MANIA OVER INTERNET STOCKS IS MIND-BOGGLING.

IT SEEMS LIKE EVERY DAY IT'S THE SAME STORY — AMAZON.COM, UP A GAJILLION POINTS... E-BAY, UP A GAJILLION POINTS... YAHOO! UP A GAJILLION POINTS...

I'M TELLING YOU, ANDY, IF I KNEW ANYTHING ABOUT THE INTERNET, I'D BE RUSHING TO START ONE OF THESE COMPANIES MYSELF SO WALL STREET COULD TURN ME INTO AN INSTANT BILLIONAIRE.

AND IF YOU KNEW ANYTHING ABOUT OUR SON, YOU WOULDN'T SAY SUCH IDEAS OUT LOUD.

OOPS.

JASON! SLOW DOWN!

HEE HEE HEE... I'M GOING TO BE RICH!

SON, ABOUT WHAT I SAID...

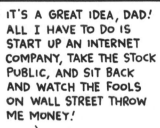

IT'S A GREAT IDEA, DAD! ALL I HAVE TO DO IS START UP AN INTERNET COMPANY, TAKE THE STOCK PUBLIC, AND SIT BACK AND WATCH THE FOOLS ON WALL STREET THROW ME MONEY!

AND THE WAY I SEE IT, MY COMPANY WOULD HAVE WHAT MOST INTERNET BUSINESSES WOULD KILL FOR.

WHAT'S THAT?

A WHOPPING ZERO PROFITS.

I SUPPOSE THAT WOULD PUT YOU PRETTY MUCH OUT IN FRONT, I ADMIT.

HEY, PETER, CAN I USE YOU AS MY FOCUS GROUP?

WHAT FOR?

I'VE COME UP WITH A NAME FOR MY INTERNET COMPANY, AND I WANT TO BOUNCE IT OFF SOMEONE TO GAUGE WALL STREET'S LIKELY REACTION.

WHAT'S THE NAME?

"JASONZONBAYHOO."

YES! YES! HE'S REACHING FOR HIS WALLET!

FOR THE DOORKNOB, LITTLE BROTHER.

"JASONZONBAYHOO"?! YOU REALLY THINK PEOPLE ARE GOING TO PAY MONEY FOR THIS STOCK?!

YOU'VE GOT NO PROFITS! NO CUSTOMERS! NO TANGIBLE WORTH OF ANY SORT!

I MEAN, WHAT'S THE DRAW??

HMM. MAYBE I SHOULD REWORK THE PROSPECTUS A LITTLE.

"JASONZONBAYHOODOTCOM." OH, MUCH IMPROVED.

SHEESH. STOP BEING SO CRITICAL AND THINK LIKE AN INVESTOR.

YOU STILL HAVEN'T TOLD ME WHAT THIS PROPOSED INTERNET COMPANY OF YOURS WILL DO.

JASONZON-BAYHOO-DOTCOM?

WILL IT HAVE A PRODUCT? CUSTOMERS? WILL IT SERVE SOME USEFUL PURPOSE?

I'LL FIGURE THAT OUT EVENTUALLY. RIGHT NOW, FIRST THINGS FIRST.

IS "INITIAL PUBLIC OFFERING" LOWERCASE?

FIRST THINGS FIRST?!?

LOOK, ONCE I'M CAPITALIZED, I'LL BUY IBM OR SOMETHING AND THE POINT'LL BE MOOT, OK?

I THOUGHT YOU WERE UP PLUGGING YOUR STOCK IN ALL THE ONLINE CHAT ROOMS.

IT'S OVER, MOM. MY INTERNET COMPANY IS AS DEAD AS A DOORNAIL.

WHAT HAPPENED?

ALL THESE INVESTOR TYPES KEPT ASKING TO SEE STUFF.

THEY CALLED YOUR BLUFF, EH?

THE ONLY THING I HAD HANDY TO SEND THEM WAS THIS ONE DINKY LITTLE PROGRAM I'D WRITTEN FOR FUN.

AND IT KILLED OFF INTEREST?

ACTUALLY, IT KILLED OFF THE INTERNET.

OUR TOP STORY TONIGHT: THE "DARTH JASON" COMPUTER VIRUS. IS THERE HOPE FOR MANKIND?

FoxTrot

by Bill Amend

 HA!

 HUH?

 OH, SHOOT. MY HOT CHOCOLATE FROZE AGAIN.

I GUESS THERE'S ONE PERK TO MOM'S KEEPING THE THERMOSTAT SO LOW.

 AAAAAA

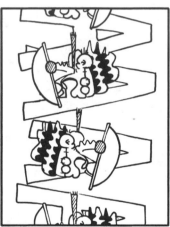

 AAAAAAA WHAM!

 YOU'RE RIGHT. IT IS JUST LIKE WITNESSING ROSWELL.

YOUR TURN.

 YES. THAT AND THE DELUXE GOLF TOWEL SET.

 HOLD ON A SEC.

 PAIGE, CAN YOU GRAB MY WALLET OFF THE COUNTER? I NEED MY CREDIT CARD NUMBER.

IT'S 24050-1081-2243-01009. EXPIRATION 06/02.

 YOU KNOW, FOR A GIRL WHO CAN'T REMEMBER HALF HER HOMEWORK ASSIGNMENTS...

I'M PRETTY SURE I SAW THESE TOWELS FOR $1.15 LESS AT THE MALL LAST SUMMER.

I CAN'T BELIEVE THIS WALL CALENDAR YOU BOUGHT, PETER.

EVERY MONTH HAS A PHOTO OF A HALF-NAKED WOMAN! GOOD LORD — MISS JULY IS MORE LIKE 99/100THS NAKED!

NEED I REMIND YOU THAT MOM AND I DO COME INTO THIS ROOM ON OCCASION? DID YOU EVER THINK OF THAT, MR. INSENSITIVE?

I MEAN, YOU COULD'VE AT LEAST GOTTEN ONE WITH A COUPLE OF HALF-NAKED MEN.

WHAT?? EVERY TIME YOU SEE ME IN MY SKIVVIES YOU JUST LAUGH.

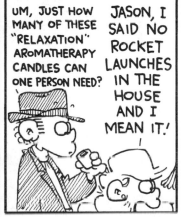

UM, JUST HOW MANY OF THESE "RELAXATION" AROMATHERAPY CANDLES CAN ONE PERSON NEED?

JASON, I SAID NO ROCKET LAUNCHES IN THE HOUSE AND I MEAN IT!

IF I'M THAT BAD ON THE RUBBER MATS, GOING ON THE ICE SHOULD PROVE INTERESTING.

JASON, GET OUT HERE — I NEED TO PRACTICE MY CHECKING.

WHAT'S THIS?

IT'S THE TEASER POSTER FOR THE UPCOMING "STAR WARS: EPISODE I." I BOUGHT IT ON THE WEB.

IT SHOWS THE YOUNG ANAKIN SKYWALKER, WHO, AS WE ALL KNOW, GROWS UP TO BECOME THE CRUEL, UNFORGIVING SYMBOL OF EVIL THROUGHOUT THE GALAXY.

NOTICE THE FOREBODING DARTH-VADER-ESQUE SHADOW HE CASTS.

ACTUALLY, I'M NOTICING MORE YOUR SCHOOL PHOTO TAPED OVER HIS FACE.

A BOY CAN DREAM, CAN'T HE?

WHAT ARE YOU DOING?

TRYING TO GROW SIDEBURNS.

BY RUBBING YOUR CHEEKS?!

I HEARD THAT BY STIMULATING THE SKIN AND GETTING CIRCULATION GOING, IT HELPS THE HAIR FOLLICLES DO THEIR THING.

SON, WHEN MOTHER NATURE IS READY FOR YOU TO GROW SIDEBURNS, IT'LL HAPPEN. RUBBING YOUR CHEEKS TO GROW HAIR IS ABOUT THE SILLIEST THING I'VE EVER —

I, UM, HAVE AN ITCH ON MY HEAD, I SWEAR.

UH-HUH.

YOU'RE DRAWING A UNICORN? EH, FIGURES.

WHAT'S THAT SUPPOSED TO MEAN?

GIRLS ALWAYS DRAW LAME-O THINGS LIKE UNICORNS. NEVER TANKS OR ROCKETS OR DINOSAUR FARMS... IT'S ALWAYS BUTTERFLIES OR RAINBOWS OR FLOWERS WITH LITTLE HAPPY FACES.

IT'S LIKE YOU HAVE SOME SORT OF GENETIC INABILITY TO DRAW THINGS THAT AREN'T CUTE.

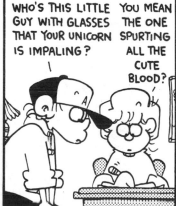

WHO'S THIS LITTLE GUY WITH GLASSES THAT YOUR UNICORN IS IMPALING?

YOU MEAN THE ONE SPURTING ALL THE CUTE BLOOD?

HEE HEE HEE...

WHAT'S SO FUNNY?

WE WERE DISSECTING EARTHWORMS IN BIOLOGY CLASS TODAY, SO I TOOK A BUNCH OF THE INNARDS HOME WITH ME IN A PLASTIC BAGGIE.

WHAT FOR?

SO I COULD PUT THEM IN JASON'S MITTENS AND GIVE THE LITTLE DWEEB A HEART ATTACK.

WHOA! COOL! WORM GUTS!

OF COURSE, I ALWAYS FORGET THAT HE'S NOT A LITTLE DWEEB.

SUPER-GARGANTUAN-MEGA ONE, AT LEAST.

I'M SO ANGRY THEY OPENED THAT COFFEEBUCKS SMACK IN THE MIDDLE OF THE OLD TOWN SQUARE.

WHY? BECAUSE IT'S SO CORPORATE?

NO...

BECAUSE OF THE PARKING CRUNCH?

NO...

BECAUSE IT'LL HURT ALL THE MOM AND POP COFFEE SHOPS?

BECAUSE IT'S RIGHT ON THE ROUTE PETER TAKES HOME FROM SCHOOL.

I WONDERED WHY HIS TEETH WERE CHATTERING ALL THROUGH DINNER.

WHERE ARE YOU GOING?

OUT TO THE DRIVEWAY TO SHOOT SOME HOOPS.

I FIGURE WITH MICHAEL JORDAN NOW RETIRED, THE NBA'S GOING TO BE IN DIRE NEED OF A NEW SUPERSTAR TO FILL THE VOID. HEY, WITH ENOUGH PRACTICE, IT COULD BE ME!

YOU'RE LOOKING AT A FAIR AMOUNT OF WORK.

NO DUH. FORTUNATELY, I HAVE A REAL PASSION FOR THE GAME.

I MEANT SHOVELING LAST NIGHT'S SNOW OFF THE DRIVE-WAY FIRST.

EH. FORGET IT, THEN.

FoxTrot
by Bill Amend

IT BOGGLES THE MIND HOW MUCH TIME YOU'VE SPENT PLAYING THAT VIDEO GAME.

IT'S THIS ONE DARN LEVEL! I CAN'T GET PAST THE RED ORB GUARDIAN!

EVERY TIME I TRY TO KILL HIM, HE SQUASHES ME FASTER THAN YOU CAN BLINK! IT'S IMPOSSIBLE! I'VE BEEN AT THIS FOR A MONTH NOW!

I SWEAR, THIS GAME IS DEFECTIVE.

THIS FROM THE BOY WITH 18 OOZING BLISTERS ON HIS THUMBS.

I'M SERIOUS. I'LL GIVE IT TWO THOUSAND MORE TRIES, THEN I'M QUITTING.

HEY! WHAT ARE YOU DOING?! I WAS IN THE MIDDLE OF A GAME!

OOPS, SORRY. I THOUGHT YOU WERE DONE.

DONE?! COULDN'T YOU SEE I WAS JUST ABOUT TO DO BATTLE WITH THE RED ORB GUARDIAN?! I JUST PAUSED IT SO I COULD GET SOME MORE SUGAR IN MY BLOODSTREAM!

THIS WAS GOING TO BE MY 10,000TH ATTEMPT! I WAS FEELING EXTRA-LUCKY! I CAN'T BELIEVE YOU RESET IT!

WHO SAID I RESET IT?

THEN WHERE'S THE RED ORB GUARDIAN? AAAA! YOU GOT PAST HIM?! HOW?! HOW?! WHAT'D YOU DO?!

WELL, LET'S SEE... THE FIRST TIME I SNEEZED, I THINK I PUSHED THIS BUTTON... OR THIS ONE...

PAIGE, I'VE BEEN TRYING TO DEFEAT THE RED ORB GUARDIAN FOR OVER A MONTH! HE'S THE TOUGHEST VIDEO GAME FOE I'VE EVER FACED!

HOW ON EARTH DID YOU GET PAST HIM?! YOU STINK!

IF YOU WANT AN ANSWER, THAT'S NO WAY TO ASK.

OK, OK, YOU DON'T STINK.

THAT'S NOT WHAT I MEANT.

HOW ON EARTH DID YOU GET PAST HIM?! MORE COOKIES?

MUCH BETTER. BUT I SAID "FRESH-BAKED."

PAIGE, I DON'T THINK YOU UNDERSTAND! I'VE SPENT HUNDREDS OF HOURS TRYING TO DEFEAT THE RED ORB GUARDIAN IN THIS VIDEO GAME!

YOU HAVE TO TELL ME HOW YOU GOT PAST HIM! YOU **HAVE** TO!

DID YOU USE THE FLAMING SWORD? THE SCREAMING SWORD? THE SWORD OF DEATH? THE SWORD OF PAIN? THE AX OF VENGEANCE? THE MACE OF MIGHT? THE RAZOR ARROWS? THE EXPLODING ARROWS? WHAT? WHAT? WHAT?

IF YOU **MUST** KNOW, I SIMPLY WALKED RIGHT BY HIM.

WELL, OF COURSE YOU DID ONCE HE WAS DEAD. WAIT! I KNOW! IT WAS THE SWORD OF FURY! AM I RIGHT?!

I DON'T THINK **YOU** UNDERSTAND, JASON...

SO THE SECRET TO GETTING PAST THE RED ORB GUARDIAN IS TO **NOT** ATTACK HIM??

BUT HE'S HUGE! HE'S NASTY! HE'S THE MOST LETHAL VIDEO GAME CREATURE EVER! HE TOWERS ABOVE YOU WITH FISTS LIKE ANVILS! SKULLS LITTER THE GROUND AT HIS FEET!

AND YOU'RE NOT SUPPOSED TO EVEN **TRY** TO TAKE THIS GUY ON IN A FIGHT??

WOW. TALK ABOUT COUNTER-INTUITIVE.

REFRESH MY MEMORY. YOU SPEND **HOW** MANY NANOSECONDS IN THE REAL WORLD EACH DAY?

WHY SO GLUM?

I SPENT AN ENTIRE MONTH TRYING TO KILL THIS ONE VIDEO GAME FOE, AND IT TURNS OUT ALL I HAD TO DO WAS WALK PAST HIM!

WHO **KNEW** YOU WEREN'T SUPPOSED TO CLUB HIM OR KICK HIM OR LOB FIRE-BALLS AT HIS HEAD, JUST BECAUSE HE'S HUGE AND FIERCE AND CAN SQUASH YOU AT WILL!

YOU'VE HEARD THE SAYING, "DISCRETION IS THE BETTER PART OF VALOR"? THINK OF THIS AS A VALUABLE LIFE LESSON.

A "LIFE LESSON"? WHO THE HECK WANTS LIFE LESSONS IN THEIR VIDEO GAMES, MOTHER!

SHEESH. NEXT THING YOU KNOW, THEY'LL TRY STICKING THEM IN THE FUNNIES.

OH, SHOOT — I LEFT THE RAW CHICKEN OUT ALL NIGHT. WELL, I'M SURE IT'S FINE...

FoxTrot
by Bill Amend

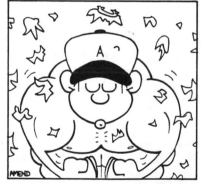

A FOUR-LETTER WORD FOR "GAPE"... YAWN.

A FIVE-LETTER WORD FOR "NIGHTTIME ANNOYANCE"... SNORE.

A THREE-LETTER WORD FOR "SLEEPY LETTERS"... ZZZ.

OH, BY THE WAY, THANKS FOR ALL YOUR HELP WITH THE CROSSWORD PUZZLE LAST NIGHT.

CROSS-WORD PUZZLE?

READY? READY.

DRAW!

PLOP! PLOP!

I KNEW WE SHOULD'VE GONE WITH THE TEN-**QUART** HATS INSTEAD.

MAYBE COWBOYS USED TO SHOOT THROUGH THESE LITTLE VENT HOLES IN THE TOP.

PETER, YOU JUST RAN A RED LIGHT.

I DID NOT. IT WAS YELLOW.

IT WAS RED!

PAIGE, I'M TELLING YOU IT WAS YELLOW!

SCREEEECH!

HONK!

OK, NOW **THAT** LIGHT WAS RED.

GREAT. MY STEREO IS DYING.

HOW DO YOU KNOW?

HOW? I'VE GOT IT CRANKED ALL THE WAY UP AND YOU CAN ONLY HEAR THE FAINTEST LITTLE BIT OF MUSIC COMING OUT OF THE SPEAKERS.

FOOL. YOU'VE GOT THE MUTE BUTTON ON. HERE.

OH, THUN DER ROAD

SEE? IT'S NOT DYING.

WHILE I'M GLAD THAT *IT'S* NOT...

HI, SWEETIE. WHAT'S FOR DINNER?

I'M GLAD YOU ASKED.

BRAISED RADISH AND BEET STEW SERVED OVER A BED OF BROWN RICE AND SESAME YOGURT.

AND IT TOOK ME ALL DAY, SO YOU'D BETTER LIKE IT.

WHY AM I NEVER GLAD I ASKED?

HERE. I HAVE A COLD. TELL ME IF IT NEEDS MORE LIMA BEAN EXTRACT.

I'LL BE RIGHT THERE, PAIGE. LET ME GRAB MY COAT.

I'VE DECIDED OUR BUYING JASON THAT GLOW-IN-THE-DARK T-SHIRT WAS LIKE THE GREATEST MOVE EVER.

I'VE ALMOST FORGOTTEN WHAT THE LITTLE SPAZ LOOKS LIKE.

FoxTrot
by Bill Amend

ALL THIS TO READ, AND CLASS IN FIVE MINUTES.

THESE KIDS ARE STARTING TO RUB OFF ON ME.

Q: A train leaves Station A at 10 a.m. and arrives 180 miles away at Station B at 2 p.m. Calculate the train's average speed for this trip.

A: Assuming that the track is straight... Assuming that the track is level... Assuming that the train stays on the track for the entire trip...

Assuming that all clocks used are synchronized... Assuming that all clocks used are accurate... Assuming that Stations A and B are in the same time zone... Assuming the times occur on the same day...

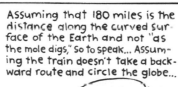

Assuming that 180 miles is the distance along the curved surface of the Earth and not "as the mole digs," so to speak... Assuming the train doesn't take a backward route and circle the globe...

Ignoring the motion of the Earth as it twirls and whizzes through space and, lastly, ignoring relativity's effects on moving clocks and observers...

45 mph.

JASON, YOU FORGOT TO PUT YOUR NAME ON YOUR HOMEWORK AGAIN.

OOPS. HOW'D YOU KNOW IT WAS MINE?

PETER, DO YOU KNOW WHAT HAPPENED TO ALL MY VALENTINE'S CHOCOLATES?

UM, NO.

JASON, DO YOU KNOW WHAT HAPPENED TO ALL MY VALENTINE'S CHOCOLATES?

UM, NO.

PAIGE, DO YOU KNOW WHAT HAPPENED TO ALL MY VALENTINE'S CHOCOLATES?

UGM, NOGE.

OPEN UP.

OGH, YOUG MEAN THEGSE CHOGOLETHS...

PRIMO COUCH POSITION... REMOTE CONTROL IN HAND... "DAWSON'S CREEK" ON IN TWO MINUTES...

LIFE DOESN'T GET MUCH BETTER THAN THIS.

YOU WATCH "DAWSON'S CREEK"?

NO. THAT'S THE POINT.

AAAA! CHANGE THE CHANNEL! MY FAVORITE SHOW IS ON!

YOU'VE GOT MAIL!

LIAR.

DAD, IF I MAY CHIME IN...

44

WATCH OUT FOR MY BUG COLLECTION, MOM!

DON'T OPEN THAT CLOSET DOOR, MOM!

LOOK OUT FOR THE BALL, MOM!

ANDYANA FOX AND THE HOUSEHOLD OF DOOM.

LOOK OUT FOR THE BALL AGAIN, MOM!

I THOUGHT YOU SAID YOU LIKED YOUR COFFEE BLACK.

I DO.

BUT THAT'S NOT BLACK. IT'S DARK BROWN.

SEE? IT'S RIGHT HERE ON THIS PANTONE CHIP: BURNT SIENNA, NUMBER PMS4625.

TELL YOU WHAT— WHY DON'T I GO ROUND UP SOME SQUID INK.

SON, PLEASE...

I GOT IT! I GOT IT!

PIFF!

IF YOU ASK ME, SNOW BASEBALL HAS SOME SERIOUS KINKS TO WORK OUT.

QUICK! MAKE A NEW BALL! HE'S HEADING FOR SECOND!

FoxTrot
by Bill Amend

THIS COMPUTER OF OURS IS SO OLD, IT'S FRIGHTENING.

YOU'VE HAD IT HOW LONG— TWO YEARS?

IT'S LIKE SOMETHING ABRAHAM LINCOLN MIGHT HAVE USED.

YOU'VE REALLY GOT TO GIVE APPLE A LOT OF CREDIT FOR PUSHING THE INDUSTRIAL DESIGN ENVELOPE.

THEIR NEW COMPUTERS AND MONITORS COME HOUSED IN COOL TRANSLUCENT PLASTICS WITH WILD COLORS AND SPACE-AGE SHAPES.

THEY JUST MADE ONE MISCALCULATION.

SOME OF US LIKE USING BORING BEIGE BOXES WITH ALL SORTS OF FAT CABLES TANGLED UP IN THE BACK.

I SWEAR, THAT THING IS SO UGLY, I DON'T EVEN WANT TO COME INTO THIS ROOM ANYMORE.

SLAM!

GOOD POINT.

SCHEME DIFFERENT.

46

PLEASE, CAN I GET A DOG, MOM? PLEASE? PLEASE? PLEASE?

I PROMISE I'LL TRAIN IT NOT TO BARK ALL NIGHT OR SOIL THE CARPET OR CHEW UP THE FURNITURE OR DIG UP YOUR GARDEN OR SHED FUR ALL OVER THE HOUSE!

PLEASE? I'VE ALWAYS WANTED A PET! WHAT DO YOU SAY?

I CAN'T BELIEVE MOM BOUGHT YOU THIS SUPER-FANCY FISH TANK.

IT'S ALL IN HOW YOU ASK.

OK, I'VE GOT THE FILTER IN... THE HEATER IN... THE ROCKS IN... THE BUBBLING CLAM SHELL IN... THE WATER IN...

...AND, OF COURSE, ALL MY CUTE LITTLE FISHIES IN.

STILL, I CAN'T HELP FEELING AS THOUGH I'VE FORGOTTEN SOMETHING.

LIKE, WHAT 15 GALLONS OF WATER WEIGHS, PERHAPS?

PETER, CAN YOU HELP ME CARRY THIS UPSTAIRS?

PAIGE, YOU'RE SUPPOSED TO FILL THE FISH TANK **AFTER** YOU TAKE IT UPSTAIRS!

HEH HEH.

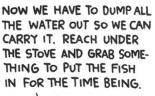

NOW WE HAVE TO DUMP ALL THE WATER OUT SO WE CAN CARRY IT. REACH UNDER THE STOVE AND GRAB SOMETHING TO PUT THE FISH IN FOR THE TIME BEING.

PER-FECT.

WE CAN PUT THE GUPPIES IN THE SAUCE PAN AND THE ANGEL FISH IN THIS BIG ONE.

DEAR, WHEN YOU SAID TONIGHT'S DINNER WAS A SURPRISE...

HERE YOU GO, FISHIES— TIME FOR DIN·DIN.

THAT'S RIGHT, LITTLE GUPPIES, EAT THE FISH FOOD...

GULP
GULP
GULP
GULP
GULP
GULP
GULP

THAT'S RIGHT, MISTER ANGEL FISH, EAT THE FISH...

GULP!

...FOOD! THE FISH FOOD! I DIDN'T FINISH THE SENTENCE!

GUPPIES REPRODUCE QUICKLY, I HOPE.

GULP! GULP! GULP!

OH, SHOOT. THE PLASTIC PLANT CAME LOOSE AGAIN.

NOW I HAVE TO STICK MY ARM IN AND FIX IT. TALK ABOUT SHEER AGONY.

THE WATER'S WARM. STOP WHINING.

IT'S NOT THE WATER THAT'S TORTURE.

ARE YOU SURE THOSE ARE GUPPIES? THEY LOOK LIKE BABY PIRANHA FISH TO ME.

SAY NO MORE.

DADDY, IF YOU MAKE THAT LAME JOKE ONE MORE TIME...

I LOVE MY AQUARIUM, MOTHER! THANK YOU!

I'M HAPPY TO HEAR THAT.

IT'S ESPECIALLY NICE TO HAVE WHEN I'M DOING MY HOMEWORK.

INTER- ESTING.

BECAUSE IT KEEPS YOU COM- PANY? BECAUSE THE SOUNDS AND COLORS ARE CALMING? BECAUSE THE MOVEMENTS OF THE FISH TAKE YOUR BRAIN INTO A HEIGHTENED STATE OF IMAGINATIVE THINKING?

BECAUSE AFTER WATCHING FISH FOR AN HOUR, EVEN GEOMETRY SEEMS EXCITING.

I'M ALWAYS GLAD TO HELP.

FoxTrot
by Bill Amend

50

PETER, I CAN'T HELP WORRYING THAT YOU'RE GETTING BEHIND IN YOUR HOMEWORK.

I'LL GET IT ALL DONE.

WHEN?! JUST LOOK AT THESE PILES OF BOOKS YOU HAVE TO READ! JUST LOOK AT THIS MOUNTAIN OF MATH PROBLEMS TO SOLVE!

MOST ALARMING IS THIS HALF-FINISHED MID-TERM ESSAY YOU'RE WRITING FOR WORLD HISTORY!

WHY'S IT SO ALARMING?

YOUR WORLD HISTORY CLASS WAS LAST SEMESTER, SON.

BY THE WAY, IT'S TWO-THIRDS FINISHED, NOT HALF.

SUPPOSEDLY, IF YOU THROW A PLAYING CARD AT THE PROPER ANGLE, IT COMES RIGHT BACK TO YOU.

WOW. FIRST TRY.

BLECCH! MOM, WHAT IS THIS?!

IT'S MILK.

IT'S SKIM MILK! YOU KNOW I HATE SKIM MILK! I LIKE WHOLE MILK!

THIS IS HEALTHIER FOR YOU.

HEALTHY-SHMEALTHY! I'M NOT DRINK-ING THIS! I WANT WHOLE MILK!

WHATEVER YOU SAY.

MY POINT WAS THAT OUR WHOLE MILK WAS WAY PAST ITS EXPIRATION.

IT STILL TASTED BETTER.

FoxTrot
by Bill Amend

PLEASE CAN'T WE GET A NEW COMPUTER?

NO.

PLEASE CAN'T WE GET A NEW COMPUTER?

NO!

PLEEEE-EEASE CAN'T WE GET A NEW COMPUTER?

JASON, NO! NOT AS LONG AS OUR CURRENT ONE WORKS!

LET ME REPHRASE THAT.

QUINCY SNUCK OUT OF HIS CAGE LAST NIGHT AND CHEWED UP AND ATE MY ENTIRE MATH TEXTBOOK.

THEN THIS MORNING HE PUKED IT UP INTO MY HAIR WHILE I WAS SLEEPING.

JASON, WHY ARE YOU TELLING ME THIS AT BREAKFAST?! DO YOU WANT ME TO THROW UP, TOO?!

FORTUNATELY, I HAD MY ENTIRE MATH TEXTBOOK MEMORIZED.

I'LL TAKE THAT AS A "YES."

ELVIS HAS LEFT THE SHOWER.

COME, JOHN BOOK — WE'RE BUILDING A BARN TODAY.

AND WHAT WOULD YOU LIKE FOR CHRISTMAS, LITTLE GIRL?

A SANE HUSBAND. JUST SHAVE.

CALL ME NANOOK.

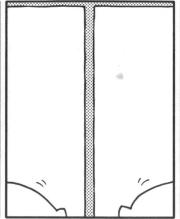

54

FoxTrot
by Bill Amend

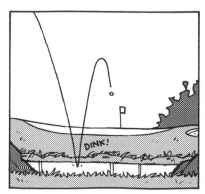

FoxTrot
by Bill Amend

I'M OFF TO BABY-SIT.

HAVE FUN. SAY HI TO MRS. O'DELL FOR ME.

I WILL. ASSUMING I CAN GET A WORD IN EDGEWISE.

HEE HEE. SHE DOES TEND TO PRATTLE ON, DOESN'T SHE?

ASSUMING **SHE** CAN GET A WORD IN EDGEWISE.

I'M CONFUSED.

I SAID I'LL BE HOME AT 8:30.

"BLUE'S CLUES"! "BLUE'S CLUES"! "BLUES CLUES"! "BLUE'S CLUES"! "BLUE'S CLUES"! "BLUE'S CLUES"!

THE PHONE MATE IS DIRTY?

KATIE MISBEHAVED MORE THAN USUAL THIS MORNING.

"BLUE'S CLUES"! "BLUE'S CLUES"! "BLUE'S CLUES"! "BLUE'S CLUES"! "BLUE'S CLUES"!

SO I TOLD HER SHE COULDN'T WATCH ANY TV OR VIDEOS TODAY WHILE YOU WERE HERE.

"BLUE'S CLUES"! "BLUE'S CLUES"! "BLUE'S CLUES"! "BLUE'S CLUES"! "BLUE'S CLUES"! "BLUE'S CLUES"! "BLUE'S CLUES"!

YOU KNOW, AS HER PUNISHMENT.

"BLUE'S CLUES"! "BLUE'S CLUES"! "BLUE'S CLUES"! "BLUE'S CLUES"!

HER PUNISHMENT?

"BLUE'S CLUES"! "BLUE'S CLUES"! "BLUE'S CLUES"! "BLUE'S CLUES"! "BLUE'S CLUES"!

SEE YOU IN FIVE HOURS.

KATIE, I'M SORRY, BUT YOUR MOTHER SAID NO TV.

"BLUE'S CLUES"! "BLUE'S CLUES"! "BLUE'S CLUES"! "BLUE'S CLUES"!

I HAVE AN IDEA. LET'S OPEN UP THIS BIG TOY CHEST OF YOURS AND TAKE YOUR MIND OFF THAT SHOW.

"BLUE'S CLUES"! "BLUE'S CLUES"! "BLUE'S CLUES"! "BLUE'S CLUES"!

OK, BAD IDEA. LET'S READ SOME OF YOUR BOOKS INSTEAD.

"BLUE'S CLUES"! "BLUE'S CLUES"! "BLUE'S CLUES"!

THIS ISN'T WHAT I THINK IT IS ON THE APPLE JUICE LABEL, IS IT?

FoxTrot
by Bill Amend

HOLD ON. I'LL GO GET HIM.

JASON, YOU HAVE A PHONE CALL.

THANKS.

WHY ANYONE WOULD WANT A CORDLESS PHONE IS BEYOND ME.

AAAA!

Tiii-iii-iii-ime, is on my side... Yes, it is...

Tiii-Tiii-Tiiime, is on my side... Yes, it is...

WHAM!

Tiii-iii-iii-ime, is on my side...

SOME ALBUMS JUST WEREN'T MEANT FOR STUDENTS.

HOW'S YOUR BIG ESSAY COMING ALONG?

MOM, WOULD IT BE OK IF I ATE THE LAST POP TART?

GO RIGHT AHEAD, PETER.

I BOUGHT TWO MORE BOXES AT THE STORE THIS MORNING.

I THINK SHE ASSUMED YOU DIDN'T KNOW THAT.

GO SEE IF WE HAVE ANOTHER GALLON OF MILK.

GLUG
GLUG
GLUG

GLUG
GLUG
GLUG

GLUG
GLUG
GLUG

I ALWAYS FORGET WHEN TO STOP.

WHAT ARE YOU DOING?

THERE'S AN ADAGE THAT SAYS A WATCHED POT NEVER BOILS.

SINCE I WANT THIS MACARONI TO COOK AS FAST AS POSSIBLE, I'M DELIBERATELY **NOT** WATCHING WHILE THE WATER HEATS UP.

ARE YOU FAMILIAR WITH THE ADAGE, "A POT ON A STOVE YOU FORGOT TO TURN ON NEVER BOILS"?

NICE TRY. YOU JUST WANT ME TO LOOK.

HOW ARE THE TAXES COMING ALONG?

MUCH BETTER THAN LAST YEAR, I CAN TELL YOU THAT.

THANK GOODNESS. I WAS AFRAID YOU HADN'T STARTED THEM YET.

I HAVEN'T.

BUT LAST YEAR I HADN'T STARTED THEM AS OF APRIL 14TH — TODAY'S ONLY THE 10TH!

FoxTrot

by Bill Amend

64

FOX, HOLD ON — DON'T TAKE BATTING PRACTICE YET. MY CAR'S IN THE PARKING LOT WHERE YOUR FOUL BALLS TEND TO LAND.

I WANT TO MOVE IT TO SOME-PLACE WHERE YOU WON'T BE LIKELY TO HIT IT.

WHY'S HE DRIVING IT INTO CENTER FIELD?

FOX, AS YOU'LL RECALL, LAST YEAR I MOVED YOU AROUND QUITE A BIT.

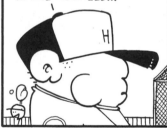

I STARTED YOU AT SECOND BASE, THEN MOVED YOU TO LEFT FIELD, THEN CENTER, THEN RIGHT, THEN BACK TO THE INFIELD, THEN BACK TO THE OUTFIELD...

WELL, THIS YEAR, SON, I WANT TO KEEP YOU IN ONE SPOT FOR THE WHOLE SEASON.

SOUNDS GOOD TO ME, COACH. WHERE?

NO SPITTING IN DUGOUT!

DON'T FEEL BAD ABOUT BEING STUCK ON THE BENCH.

LOOK AT IT THE WAY I DO — AS AN OPPORTUNITY TO STUDY THE GAME WITHOUT THE ANNOYING DISTRACTION OF HAVING TO PLAY IT.

IF YOU ASK ME, DUGOUT DUTY IS HIGHLY UNDERRATED.

GOLDTHWAIT, GET OUT HERE! YOU'RE BATTING CLEANUP! LET'S GO!

SERIOUSLY. CHEER UP.

FoxTrot
by Bill Amend

67

DAD'S COMING TO THE BASE-BALL GAME?!

IT WAS SUPPOSED TO BE A SURPRISE, BUT YES.

HE MOVED UP A MEETING SO HE COULD GET OUT OF WORK EARLY.

I WISH I COULD JOIN HIM — THE WEATHERMAN SAID IT'S GOING TO BE A GLORIOUS DAY.

TRUST ME. IT WON'T BE.

SAY, YOU NEVER TOLD US WHAT POSITION YOU'RE PLAYING.

DAD'S COMING TO THE GAME TODAY.

SO?

SO HE'S GOING TO SIT THERE EVERY INNING AND SEE ME — HIS OLDEST SON, HIS BASEBALL PROTÉGÉ — WARMING THE BENCH IN THE DUGOUT!

I'M NEVER GOING TO BE ABLE TO FACE HIM AGAIN. I'LL BE SO EMBARRASSED.

PETER, THIS IS DAD WE'RE TALKING ABOUT.

HE WON'T BE DISAPPOINTED?

HE WON'T NOTICE.

I GOT STUCK IN TRAFFIC. DID I MISS ANYTHING?

JUST THE FIRST INNING.

HEY, WHY'S PETER SITTING IN THE DUGOUT WHEN HIS TEAM'S OUT IN THE FIELD? I ALWAYS ASSUMED HE WAS THE STAR OF THE SQUAD — WHAT DOES THIS MEAN??

THINK ABOUT IT FOR A SEC, DAD. IT'LL DAWN ON YOU.

AIEEE! HE GOT HURT? AND I WASN'T HERE?!?

APPARENTLY, THIS "SEC" MAY TAKE A WHILE. LET ME RE-FILL MY SODA.

IT'S THE LAST INNING AND PETER HASN'T PLAYED AT ALL.

HE'S JUST SAT THERE ON THE BENCH. THE COACH DOESN'T EVEN LOOK LIKE HE WOULD **CONSIDER** PUT-TING PETER IN THE GAME.

DOES THIS MEAN WHAT I THINK IT MEANS?

'FRAID SO, DAD.

MY SON'S IN THE STARTING PITCHER ROTATION!

I WISH YOU WOULDN'T MAKE ME CHOKE WHILE I'M EATING A HOT DOG.

PETER FOX! YOU DA MAN!

DADDY, I DON'T KNOW HOW TO TELL YOU THIS GENTLY.

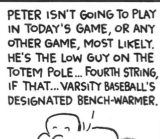

PETER ISN'T GOING TO PLAY IN TODAY'S GAME, OR ANY OTHER GAME, MOST LIKELY. HE'S THE LOW GUY ON THE TOTEM POLE... FOURTH STRING, IF THAT... VARSITY BASEBALL'S DESIGNATED BENCH-WARMER.

YOU JUST **ASSUMED** HE WAS A STAR. THE TRUTH IS HE'S NOT.

PETER FOX! YOU DA MAN!

DADDY, DON'T BE SO CLUE-LESS. YOU ACT LIKE NOTHING'S CHANGED.

I CAN'T BELIEVE DAD CHEERED ME ON LIKE THAT TODAY.

I MEAN, EVEN AFTER HE SAW I WAS JUST A BENCH-WARMER, A FOURTH-STRING-ER, A **NOBODY**, HE KEPT RIGHT ON YELLING, "RAH, RAH, PETER! RAH, RAH, PETER!"

I THOUGHT FOR SURE HE'D THINK I WAS A FAILURE. I THOUGHT FOR SURE HE'D BE DISAPPOINTED.

SOMETIMES OUR DAD'S PRETTY COOL.

FOR A GUY WHO SAYS "RAH."

FoxTrot
by Bill Amend

DARN IT. STILL 24 DAYS LEFT.

I NEED A FASTER WATCH.

Welcome to the Jason Fox **STAR WARS** EPISODE I Rumors Web Page!!!

Greetings, fellow "Star Wars" fans! With less than four weeks to go before the big event, new details about the movie are leaking out faster than a Tatooine pod race!

Spoilers ahead! Beware!

First, confirmation of last week's report here that John Williams' score departs rather drastically from his earlier SW works. "He's sort of big on kazoos now," states one well-placed insider. Another source would only characterize the new sound as "highly experimental."

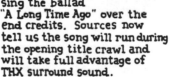

Speaking of music, we erred in our earlier report that "Titanic's" own Celine Dion would sing the ballad "A Long Time Ago" over the end credits. Sources now tell us the song will run during the opening title crawl and will take full advantage of THX surround sound.

Bad news for special effects fans. Apparently stung by criticism from his mailman that the trailers looked "too digital," George Lucas has ordered all computer-generated images removed from the film. CGI character Jar Jar Binks will reportedly be renamed "Jar Jar Binks, Master of Invisibility."

Finally, rumors continue to swirl of a last-minute voice recasting. A number of spies report that fitness guru Richard Simmons has been hired to rerecord all of lead villain Darth Maul's dialogue. "We think audiences will be surprised at how well he growls," says one Skywalker Ranch informant.

LIE ALL YOU WANT—YOU STILL WON'T BE ABLE TO BUY TICKETS OPENING DAY.

OH, YE OF LITTLE FAITH.

..."wall-to-wall Ewoks," was the reaction of a source privy to the...

71

FoxTrot
by Bill Amend

Panel 1:
I SWEAR, THIS WARM WEATHER HAD BETTER END BEFORE FINALS.

WHY'S THAT?

Panel 2:
IT MAKES STUDYING NEXT TO IMPOSSIBLE, THAT'S WHY!

Panel 3:
PAIGE, PART OF GROWING UP IS LEARNING TO OVERCOME THINGS LIKE THE TEMPTATION TO GOOF OFF JUST BECAUSE IT'S NICE OUT.

Panel 4:
I'M TALKING ABOUT JASON AND HIS NEED TO THROW WATER BALLOONS.

THIS RED SOGGY PULP IS YOUR BINDER?!

Panel 5:
JUST THINK, MOM — IF WE GOT A SECOND COMPUTER, WE COULD NETWORK IT WITH OUR CURRENT ONE AND PLAY HEAD-TO-HEAD VIDEO GAMES DAY AND NIGHT ALL SUMMER LONG!

Panel 6:
WHADDYA SAY? TELL ME THAT'S NOT WORTH $1,000 OR MORE!

Panel 7:
(no dialogue)

Panel 8:
SOME FOCUS GROUP YOU TURNED OUT TO BE.

DID YOU TELL HER ABOUT THE ONE WITH BUILT-IN TWIN SUBWOOFERS?

Panel 9:
NICOLE WAS TELLING ME TODAY HOW HER MOM SERVED LEFTOVERS FOR FOUR DAYS STRAIGHT.

FASH!

Panel 10:
I TOLD HER I COULDN'T UNDERSTAND THAT.

HER MOM WAS PROBABLY BUSY. YOU TRY COOKING DINNER EVERY NIGHT.

Panel 11:
NO, NO — I COULDN'T UNDERSTAND WHAT A "LEFTOVER" WAS.

I ALWAYS FORGET YOU'VE NEVER KNOWN LIFE WITHOUT PETER.

MOM, ANY CHANCE YOU COULD MAKE AN EXTRA MEAT LOAF TONIGHT?

FASH!

JASON, PLEASE SEE ME AFTER CLASS.

I DON'T UNDERSTAND— I WROTE "STEALTH FIGHTER" ON THIS PLANE AS DAY.

JASON, WHY ARE YOU IN THE GARBAGE CAN?

I'M HIDING FROM PAIGE.

I PUT A SNAIL IN HER BOOK BAG, WHICH NATURALLY DIDN'T GO OVER VERY WELL.

I FIGURE IF I BURY MYSELF UNDER THESE BANANA PEELS AND USED COFFEE FILTERS, SHE'LL NEVER FIND ME AND EVENTUALLY WILL GIVE UP LOOKING.

ISN'T IT GREAT THE WAY OUR BROTHER PUNISHES HIMSELF FOR US?

WHAT DO YOU THINK— SIX MORE HOURS UNTIL I GIVE UP LOOKING?

PAIGE, YOU'VE HAD THAT PONYTAIL FOR AS LONG AS I CAN REMEMBER.

SO?

HAVE YOU EVER CONSIDERED CUTTING IT OFF? YOU KNOW, GOING WITH SHORT HAIR FOR A CHANGE?

NOT REALLY.

NEVER?

NO, WHY?

UM...

SAY, WHAT HAPPENED TO ALL THAT GUM YOU WERE CHEWING?

FoxTrot
by Bill Amend

I LIKE THE IDEA OF THEM LINING UP TO SEE ME.

SCRITCH SCRITCH SCRITCH

LOTTERY SCRATCHERS?? GOOD LORD.

TALK ABOUT YOUR WASTE OF MONEY. TALK ABOUT YOUR WASTE OF TIME.

TALK ABOUT YOUR SUCKER BETS.

WOO HOO! I WON $5!

I GET HALF.

THESE ONLINE AUCTION SITES ARE INCREDIBLE, PETER!

I MEAN, LOOK AT THESE PRICES: A PINK DRESS, $3!... A YELLOW SILK BLOUSE, $2!... A CUDDLES THE KITTEN WRISTWATCH, $2.75!

I COULD REALLY GET HOOKED ON THIS.

I SUPPOSE IF YOU LIKE BUYING GIRLS' CLOTHING.

WHO'S BUYING?

HAS ANYONE SEEN MY WATCH?

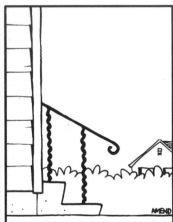

FoxTrot

by Bill Amend

FoxTrot
by Bill Amend

82

(YAWN)

WE DIDN'T THINK YOU'D **EVER** WAKE UP.

I ALWAYS LIKE TO SLEEP IN ON THE FIRST DAY OF SUMMER VACATION. I THINK I'VE EARNED THE RIGHT.

WHAT TIME IS IT, BY THE WAY?

ALMOST NOON.

EH, THAT'S NOT SO LATE.

...ON THE **THIRD** DAY OF SUMMER VACATION.

NO, SON, YOUR MOTHER — AND I WON'T HELP YOU POD RACE.

PHOOEY.

BRUSH BRUSH BRUSH

FLOSS FLOSS FLOSS

COMB COMB COMB

YOU KNOW, YOU **COULD** JUST USE A MIRROR.

MY JASONCAM WEB SITE NEEDS THE TRAFFIC.

FoxTrot
by Bill Amend

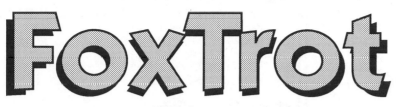

DAD SAYS YOU'RE GOING BACK TO WORK AT THE MOVIE THEATER. | YEAH. I'M NOT REALLY LOOKING FORWARD TO IT, THOUGH.

WHY? I THOUGHT YOU LIKED WORKING THERE. | THAT WAS LAST SUMMER. THINGS HAVE CHANGED SINCE THEN.

WHAT'S DIFFERENT? THE MANAGEMENT? THE PAY? THE HOURS? | "STAR WARS" WASN'T PLAYING THEN.

AH. | ...ON ALL 22 SCREENS. | I SENSE MUCH FEAR IN YOU.

NOW, PETER, THE THING TO KEEP IN MIND WITH THESE "STAR WARS" FANS IS THEY'RE JUST ORDINARY PEOPLE, MOSTLY.

SURE, THEY LIKE TO DRESS UP IN COSTUMES. AND WAVE PLASTIC LIGHTSABERS. AND GIVE STANDING OVATIONS TO THE LUCASFILM LOGO. AND SLEEP ON SIDEWALKS FOR TICKETS.

BUT OTHER THAN THAT, THEY REALLY ARE JUST LIKE YOU AND ME.

AT LAST WE WILL REVEAL OURSELVES TO THE RESTROOM. | ...ONLY INSANE. | MR. MAUL, SIR? YOU DROPPED YOUR STRAW.

HI. I'D LIKE SIX TICKETS FOR "THE PHANTOM MENACE" ON YOUR BIGGEST SCREEN. | FOR WHICH SHOW TIME?

WHAT DO YOU MEAN, WHICH SHOW TIME? | THERE ARE SIX SHOW TIMES — 11:30, 2:00, 4:30, 7:00, 9:30 AND MIDNIGHT.

RIGHT. I WANT ONE TICKET FOR EACH SCREENING. | OH.

YOU MUST BE NEW. I DIDN'T SEE YOU HERE YESTERDAY. | YOU MAY NOT SEE ME HERE TOMORROW, EITHER.

THAT COMES TO $13.75.

I BELIEVE A DOLLAR WILL BE SUFFICIENT.

HUH?

A DOLLAR WILL BE SUFFICIENT.

HE SAID A DOLLAR *WILL* BE SUFFICIENT.

GUYS, THERE'S A REALLY LONG LINE BEHIND YOU.

SMART OF THEM TO HIRE PEOPLE IMMUNE TO JEDI MIND TRICKS.

SOMEONE *WILL* LEND US $12.75...

SO WHAT ALIEN CREATURE ARE YOU SUPPOSED TO BE?

I'M A BANTHA.

SO WHAT ALIEN CREATURE ARE YOU SUPPOSED TO BE?

I'M BIB FORTUNA.

SO WHAT ALIEN CREATURE ARE YOU SUPPOSED TO BE?

I NEED TO STOP RUNNING ON AUTOPILOT.

FOR THE RECORD, *MY* KI-ADI-MUNDI WIG IS BETTER.

EXSQUEEZE ME! MESA NEED HELP FINDING THEATER 15!

I WILL NOT CONDONE A COURSE OF ACTION THAT WILL PUT BUTTER ON MY POPCORN.

BEGIN SEATING YOUR TROOPS.

IT'S GOING TO BE A LONG SUMMER.

WE'LL BE WATCHING YOUR CAREER WITH GREAT INTEREST.

FoxTrot
by Bill Amend

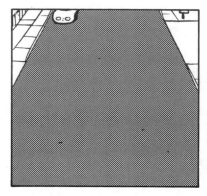

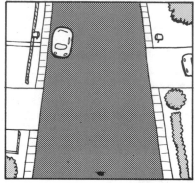

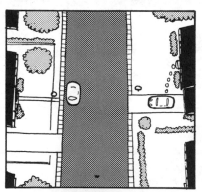

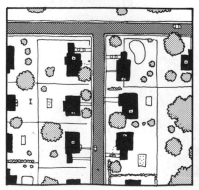

FOX, I NEED YOU TO FLY OUT TO BOONHURST TOMORROW TO WRAP UP THAT DEAL WITH GERNANDCO.

YOU'VE BEEN MY RIGHT-HAND MAN ON THIS PROJECT, WHICH IS WHY I'M SENDING YOU.

THIS CLIENT DEMANDS THE HIGHEST LEVEL OF ATTENTION WE CAN GIVE.

AND, SEEING AS I'M SURE AS HECK NOT FLYING INTO BOONHURST...

DO YOU KNOW IF THEY'VE FINISHED PAVING THE RUNWAY YET?

ANDY, I'M GOING ON A **BUSINESS** TRIP! IT'S NOT LIKE SOME SORT OF VACATION!

I HAVE TO FLY OUT AT 6 A.M. TOMORROW, GO TO A BUNCH OF MEETINGS, STAY AT SOME FLEABAG MOTEL, AND THEN FLY HOME AT 6 A.M. THE NEXT DAY!

SURE, YOU'LL BE STUCK HERE ALONE WITH THE KIDS, BUT IT'S NOT LIKE **I'M** GOING TO BE LEAPING WITH JOY!

CERTAINLY NOT WITH THAT HEAVY GOLF BAG.

THE **CLIENT** ASKED ME TO BRING IT! DON'T BLAME **ME**!

HI. I'M ON THE 6 A.M. FLIGHT TO BOONHURST.

I'M AFRAID THERE'S BEEN A SCHEDULE CHANGE.

SECURITY NOTICE

THAT FLIGHT WAS MOVED TO A 10:30 DEPARTURE TIME. YOU REALLY SHOULD CALL IN ADVANCE TO DOUBLE-CHECK THESE THINGS.

YOU CAN'T DO THIS! I'LL BE LATE FOR A MEETING!

SIR, WE HAVE THE RIGHT TO CHANGE OUR SCHEDULES. IT SAYS SO ON THE TICKET.

GREAT. NOW I'M STUCK HERE FOR 4½ HOURS.

PERHAPS I WASN'T CLEAR. YOUR FLIGHT LEFT AT 10:30 LAST NIGHT.

SECURITY NOTICE

YOU DON'T HAVE ANY OTHER FLIGHTS TO BOONHURST?!

CALM DOWN, SIR. I'M SURE WE CAN GET YOU THERE.

NOTICE TO PASSENGERS

AH, HERE WE GO. I CAN ROUTE YOU THROUGH CHICAGO, THEN TO DALLAS, THEN TO LOS ANGELES, THEN TO ATLANTA, THEN TO PORTLAND, THEN TO DENVER, THEN TO CHARLOTTE, THEN TO BOONHURST.

DARE I ASK WHEN I'LL GET THERE?

LET'S SEE... 3:25 P.M.

NOTICE TO PASSENGERS

I GUESS THAT'S NOT TOO BAD.

... NEXT TUESDAY.

NOTICE TO PASSENGERS

AMEND

THERE HAS BEEN A GATE CHANGE. FLIGHT 1313 WILL NOW DEPART FROM GATE C135.

THERE HAS BEEN A GATE CHANGE. FLIGHT 1313 WILL NOW DEPART FROM GATE B2.

THERE HAS BEEN A GATE CHANGE. FLIGHT 1313 WILL NOW DEPART FROM GATE D496.

THERE'S A GENTLE-MAN WHO WANTS TO KNOW IF WE GIVE FREQUENT-FLIER POINTS FOR MILES TRAVELED IN THE AIRPORT.

CORREC-TION: Z496.

AAAA!

BOARDING AT 705

AMEND

GOOD MORNING, LADIES AND GENTLEMEN. WE'D LIKE TO BEGIN BY PRE-BOARDING ANY FAMILIES TRAVELING WITH INFANTS OR SMALL CHILDREN.

GATE

OK, ROWS 25-36 MAY NOW BOARD. ROWS 19-36 MAY NOW BOARD. ROWS 14-36 MAY NOW BOARD.

GATE

ROWS 1-12 MAY NOW BOARD. ALSO, ROW 13, SEATS A, B, D, E AND F.

GATE

THANK YOU. THE REMAINING PAS-SENGER MAY NOW BOARD AT HIS LEISURE.

I KNEW I SHOULDN'T HAVE CALLED HIM A STEWARDESS.

GATE

AMEND

UM, THERE SEEMS TO BE A PROBLEM WITH THE ANGLE OF MY SEAT BACK.

HERE. I CAN FIX THAT.

YOU HAD IT RECLINED.

I'M PAYING **HOW** MUCH TO FLY WITH YOU PEOPLE?

OH, NO THANKS.

ARE YOU ALLERGIC TO PEANUTS?

NO, NO — IT'S JUST THAT THESE SNACK FOOD THINGS ALWAYS SPOIL MY APPETITE. I WANT TO BE GOOD AND HUNGRY, SINCE I IMAGINE THERE'LL BE LUNCH ON THIS FLIGHT.

YOU'RE RIGHT.

THERE'S LUNCH?

YOU'RE IMAGINING IT.

MAN, THESE PEANUTS ARE SALTY.

THE DRINK CART WILL BE BY IN TWO HOURS.

HERE YOU GO, SIR.

YES!

YESSS!

YESSSSS!

I TOLD YOU, ONLY GIVE FULL CANS TO PASSENGERS WHO CAN HANDLE IT.

SIR, WE DON'T ALLOW STANDING ON SEATS.

GOOD MORNING, LADIES AND GENTLEMEN. TODAY'S VIDEO PRESENTATION WILL BE THE 1993 FILM "ALIVE."

IT'S THE HARROWING TRUE STORY OF HOW AN AIRPLANE CRASH LEFT ITS SURVIVORS ALONE AND FORCED TO EAT THEIR DEAD.

THIS MOVIE WILL BE SHOWN FREE OF CHARGE.

EARPLUGS AND BLINDERS ARE $20. YOU GUYS ARE GETTING SMART.

HELLO, EVERYONE. THIS IS THE CAPTAIN SPEAKING.

I JUST WANT TO DRAW YOUR ATTENTION TO THE VIEW OUT THE LEFT SIDE OF THE AIRCRAFT. WE'LL BE PASSING OVER THE GRAND CANYON SHORTLY, AND IT'S AN ABSOLUTELY BEAUTIFUL SIGHT.

THINK OF THIS AS YOUR REWARD FOR CHOOSING TO TRAVEL WITH US TODAY.

NATURALLY, THIS FLIGHT FROM CHICAGO TO BOSTON WILL BE GETTING IN A LITTLE LATER THAN SCHEDULED.

WELCOME TO BOONHURST, LADIES AND GENTLEMEN.

BAGGAGE CLAIM IS TO YOUR LEFT.

ANSPORTATION   PARKING
Roger Fox

YOU DON'T HAVE TO TELL ME IT WAS A LONG FLIGHT. MIND IF I CALL IN? WE HAD A POOL ON WHAT DAY YOU'D ARRIVE.

ANDY? KIDS? I'M HOME!

HI DADDY. HOW WAS YOUR TRIP?

UGGH. YOU WOULD NOT **BELIEVE** THE SHEER AGONY OF IT ALL.

AIRLINE DELAYS... MISSED CONNECTIONS... AN OVERBOOKED HOTEL... I SWEAR, LIFE DOESN'T GET ANY WORSE THAN A BUSINESS TRIP TO BOONHURST. WHERE'S YOUR MOTHER?

SHE HAD TO TAKE JASON TO THE HOSPITAL.

WHAT? IS HE DOING VOLUNTEER WORK OR SOMETHING?

I GOT HERE AS SOON AS I COULD! HOW IS HE?

HE'S FINE. HE NEEDED THREE STITCHES IN HIS CHIN.

PAIGE TOLD ME WHAT HAPPENED! THANK GOD HE'S ALL RIGHT! THANK GOD HE WASN'T KILLED!

EMERGENCY

I CAN'T BELIEVE OUR LITTLE JASON WAS HIT BY A CAR!

THAT'S WHAT PAIGE TOLD YOU?

EMERGENCY

WELL, SHE SAID SOME OTHER STUFF, TOO, BUT I WAS RUNNING OUT THE DOOR. WHY?

ARE YOU FAMILIAR WITH THE "HOT WHEELS" LINE OF VEHICLES?

JASON! SON! ARE YOU OK?! YOUR MOTHER TOLD ME WHAT HAPPENED!

HOSPITAL DIRECTORY

I'M SO SORRY I WASN'T THERE WHEN YOU GOT HURT! I'M SO SORRY I WASN'T AT HOME!

NCY

HOSP DIRE

ROGER, IF YOU SQUEEZE HIM ANY TIGHTER, HIS STITCHES MAY BURST.

WHOOPS

WHOA— DO IT IN FRONT OF A MIRROR. I WANT TO SEE.

SO WHAT'S THE VERDICT?

THREE STITCHES.

POOR GUY. WELL, LET ME KNOW IF THERE'S ANYTHING I CAN DO FOR YOU.

YOU COULD LET ME TAKE THE BANDAGE OFF AND SHOW THEM TO YOU.

ICK. I'D PROBABLY PUKE.

THAT'S THE IDEA.

LET ME KNOW IF THERE'S ANYTHING SANE I CAN DO FOR YOU.

ALL TALK. I SHOULD HAVE KNOWN IT.

I'VE HAD TO GET STITCHES, TOO, YOU KNOW.

THERE WAS THE TIME I SWUNG A 9-IRON INTO MY HEAD... THE TIME I DID A BACK FLIP ONTO THE LOWENSTEIN'S DIVING BOARD... AND, OF COURSE, THE TIME I SKATEBOARDED INTO A STONE WALL.

... BLINDFOLDED. OUCH.

ANYWAY, SO I'M STILL WAY COOLER THAN YOU.

I'M YOUNG. GIVE ME TIME.

I CAN'T BELIEVE I WASN'T HERE WHEN JASON GOT HURT.

HE'S FINE. STOP BEATING YOURSELF UP.

BUT WHAT IF IT HAD BEEN MORE SERIOUS?! WHAT IF IT HAD BEEN A REAL CAR THAT HIT HIM AND NOT JUST A TOY ONE?! THERE I WAS OFF ON SOME IDIOTIC BUSINESS TRIP!

I WASN'T AROUND WHEN MY LITTLE BOY NEEDED ME! I WASN'T AROUND WHEN MY LITTLE BOY WAS HURT!

ROGER, YOU CAN'T SPEND 24 HOURS A DAY HOVERING OVER YOUR KIDS! WHAT ARE YOU GOING TO DO? QUIT YOUR JOB?!

NOW THERE'S A THOUGHT.

I WAS KIDDING, ROGER. KIDDING!

FoxTrot
by Bill Amend

FoxTrot
by Bill Amend

YOU QUIT YOUR JOB?? ARE YOU INSANE??

ANDY, IT WAS MY JOB THAT WAS INSANE!

I'VE BEEN GIVING OLD MAN PEMBROOK 10 HOURS OF MY LIFE FOR EVERY TWO OR THREE I GIVE MY FAMILY! THAT'S NUTS! AND I TOLD HIM THAT, TOO!

I CAN'T WAIT TO HEAR THE KIDS' REACTION WHEN I TELL THEM HOW MUCH MORE TIME WE'LL HAVE TOGETHER.

YOU QUIT YOUR JOB?? ARE YOU INSANE??

WHO'S UP FOR A GAME OF FREEZE TAG?!

I'VE CHANGED MY MIND. I THINK IT'S GREAT THAT YOU'VE QUIT YOUR JOB.

YOU DO?

ABSOLUTELY. I THINK IT'S WONDERFUL THAT YOU WANT TO SPEND MORE TIME WITH YOUR FAMILY EVEN THOUGH IT MEANS LETTING 25 YEARS OF EXPERIENCE AND HARD WORK IN THE CORPORATE WORLD GO TO WASTE FOR WHO KNOWS HOW LONG WHILE WE EAT UP OUR SAVINGS.

I'M BEHIND YOU 100 PERCENT.

THANKS, SWEETIE. NOW I KNOW IT WAS THE RIGHT DECISION.

BOY, WHEN REVERSE PSYCHOLOGY BACK-FIRES, IT REALLY BACKFIRES.

HEY, SON—TEACH ME HOW TO PLAY THOSE VIDEO GAMES OF YOURS.

DO YOU REALIZE I'D BEEN WORKING NON-STOP FOR PEMBROOK SINCE COLLEGE?

I DIDN'T JUST QUIT THIS WEEK, I SET MYSELF FREE!

FREE TO READ! FREE TO WRITE! FREE TO TRAVEL! FREE TO STUDY! FREE TO DANCE! TO SING! TO FINALLY LIVE THIS THING CALLED LIFE!

WELL, YOU'D BETTER GET STARTED, THEN.

I THOUGHT I'D TAKE A NAP FIRST.

DADDY REALLY QUIT HIS JOB?

YUP.

WHAT'S HE GOING TO DO?

WHO KNOWS. HIS PLAN IS TO SPEND MORE TIME HERE AT HOME.

I JUST PRAY HE'LL WISE UP AND GO BACK TO WORK.

BEFORE WE END UP IN THE POOR-HOUSE?

TRY THE NUT-HOUSE.

WHOOPS. KIDS, WHAT WAS YOUR SECOND CHOICE FOR LUNCH?

HEY, KIDS, SEEING AS YOU'RE OUT OF SCHOOL AND I'VE QUIT MY JOB, I THOUGHT WE COULD SPEND THE SUMMER DOING FUN THINGS TOGETHER!

WE COULD HANG OUT TOGETHER AT THE MALL... HANG OUT TOGETHER AT THE ICE CREAM PARLOR... HANG OUT TOGETHER AT THE POOL...

COULD WE PLAY A GAME FIRST?

HIDE-AND-SEEK? EXCELLENT CHOICE.

HEY, PETE — CARE TO HIT SOME BALLS?

NOT NOW, DAD. I'M GOING OVER TO DENISE'S.

HEY, PAIGE — CARE TO PLAY SOME CARDS?

NOT NOW, DADDY. I'M WATCHING TV.

HEY, JASON — CARE TO HELP ME EAT THESE COOKIES?

NOT NOW, DAD. I'M CALIBRATING MY ROCKET FINS.

HMM. THIS ISN'T QUITE THE "CARE-FREE" LIFE I HAD IN MIND.

ASK ME IF I CARE THAT YOU QUIT WORKING, DEAR.

FoxTrot
by Bill Amend

ROGER, I'M GLAD QUITTING YOUR JOB MAKES YOU HAPPY, BUT THERE IS THE LITTLE MATTER OF MONEY.

DO YOU HAVE ANY IDEA HOW FAST WE'LL EAT THROUGH OUR SAVINGS WITH YOU NOT WORKING?

MY LITTLE NEWSPAPER SALARY JUST ISN'T ENOUGH TO LIVE ON.

ANDY, RELAX. WE'VE GOT IT ALL FIGURED OUT.

"WE"?

THE GUY ON THE INFOMERCIAL AND ME.

YOU GOT SUCKED IN BY AN INFOMERCIAL?! ROGER, WHAT WERE YOU THINKING?!

I WANT YOU TO BE AS FILTHY RICH AS I AM!

"THE WILLY MILLIONS RAGS-TO-RICHES HOME-STUDY PROGRAM"?!

LET ME SHOW YOU THE MONEY FOR ONLY $199.95!

YOU PAID $200?!?

CALL TODAY!

ARE YOU SURE THIS ISN'T THE COMEDY CHANNEL WE'RE WATCHING?

WILL YOU CALM DOWN? THE THING HAS A 30-DAY MONEY-BACK GUARANTEE.

ALLOW 31 DAYS FOR SHIPPING.

DAD, THIS CAME IN THE MAIL FOR YOU.

OH?

OOO — IT'S FROM THE WILLY MILLIONS FOUNDATION! IT MUST BE A NOTE TELLING ME MY COMPREHENSIVE HOME-STUDY COURSE IN WEALTH ACCUMULATION IS ON ITS WAY!

WELL, THIS IS RATHER DISAPPOINTING.

YOUR SHIPMENT'S BEEN DELAYED?

THIS, UM, IS THE SHIPMENT.

ACCORDING TO THE WILLY MILLIONS "ROAD TO FILTHY RICHES" BOOKLET, THE SECRET TO FINANCIAL FREEDOM IS FAIRLY STRAIGHTFORWARD.

"STEP 1 — CREATE A PRODUCT TO SELL FOR $200. STEP 2 — GET 5,000 PEOPLE TO BUY IT. STEP 3 — UNCORK THE CHAMPAGNE, YOU'RE NOW A MILLIONAIRE."

UNFORTUNATELY, IT DOESN'T GO INTO ANY REAL DETAIL.

YOU'D THINK THIS WOULD AT LEAST INCLUDE AN **EXAMPLE** OF A PRODUCT.

THAT BOOKLET COST YOU, WHAT, $199.95?

I'M SUCH AN IDIOT!

HERE I AM WITH NO JOB, AND I'M SPENDING $200 I CAN'T AFFORD FOR A BOOKLET ABOUT PERSONAL WEALTH!

WILLY MILLIONS IS NOTHING MORE THAN A TWO-BIT SCAM ARTIST HIDING BEHIND A FLASHY INFOMERCIAL!

I HAVE A GOOD MIND TO ATTEND HIS $800 LIVE SEMINAR AND TELL HIM TO HIS FACE!

I CAN'T BELIEVE WHAT A FOOL I WAS.

I ACTUALLY BELIEVED THAT STUPID WILLY MILLIONS INFOMERCIAL! I ACTUALLY BELIEVED I COULD MAKE MONEY WITHOUT LIFTING A FINGER!

WELL, I'VE LEARNED MY LESSON. STARTING MONDAY, I'LL BE LIFTING THESE FINGERS LIKE CRAZY.

YOU'RE GOING BACK TO WORK?!

BETTER — I'LL BE DAY TRADING STOCKS ON THE INTERNET.

ABOUT YOUR BELIEF THAT YOU **WERE** A FOOL...

OK, DAD, THE COMPUTER'S HOOKED UP IN YOUR BEDROOM!

FoxTrot
by Bill Amend

DAY TRADING STOCKS IS GOING TO MAKE US RICH, JASON. LET'S GET STARTED.

DID YOU WANT TO REVIEW THE FUNDAMENTALS FIRST, MAYBE?

I KNOW, I KNOW. BUY LOW, SELL HIGH... DON'T LEAVE OPEN POSITIONS OVERNIGHT... STAY CALM, DON'T PANIC...

I MEANT ABOUT HOW TO WORK MOM'S COMPUTER.

(Beep) REFORMATING HARD DRIVE.

STAY CALM... DON'T PANIC...

I SET YOUR E-LYNCHITY BROKERAGE ACCOUNT UP SO YOU CAN TRADE ON MARGIN.

WHAT'S THAT MEAN?

IT MEANS YOU CAN BUY STOCKS GALORE WITH BORROWED MONEY AND AFTER THE STOCKS SHOOT UP, YOU POCKET THE PROFITS. IT'S FOOLPROOF!

UNLESS THE STOCKS GO DOWN, THAT IS.

STOCKS CAN GO DOWN?

HELLO, E-LYNCHITY? IS THERE SOMEONE I COULD SPEAK WITH WHO WAS BORN BEFORE THE '90s?

I'M TELLING YOU, DAD, STOCKS DON'T GO DOWN.

THE STOCK PRICE IS DOWN! QUICK, DAD, **BUY!**

CLICK

THE STOCK PRICE IS UP! QUICK, DAD, **SELL!**

CLICK

TRY DAY TRADING WITH MY JOY-STICK. ITS BUTTONS RESPOND A HAIR FASTER.

THESE RED NUMBERS IN PARENTHESES MEAN I **MADE** MONEY, RIGHT?

FoxTrot
by Bill Amend

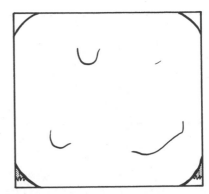

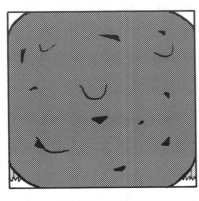

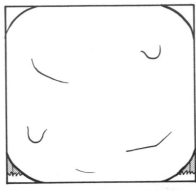

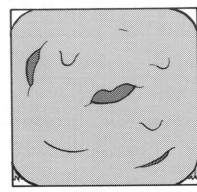

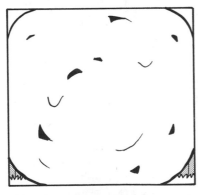

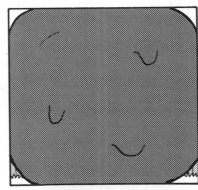

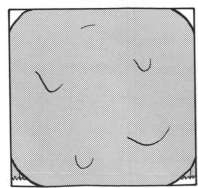

AND PEOPLE THINK **AUTUMN** IS THE MOST COLORFUL SEASON.

THAT'S WHAT? YOUR TWELFTH CONE TODAY?

AMEND

POOR UNEMPLOYED DAD.

POOR, POOR UNEMPLOYED DAD.

POOR, POOR, POOR, POOR, POOR, POOR, POOR, POOR, POOR, POOR—

JASON, WILL YOU KNOCK IT OFF?! I QUIT MY JOB ON PURPOSE. I DON'T NEED YOUR PITY!

PITY? I'M JUST TALKING FINANCES.

REMIND ME AGAIN WHY I WANTED TO SPEND MORE TIME WITH MY FAMILY...

MAYBE THIS EARLY RETIREMENT THING WAS ALL A BIG MISTAKE.

MAYBE MY DESIRE TO HANG OUT WITH MY CHILDREN SHOULD HAVE BEEN BALANCED WITH MY RESPONSIBILITY TO PROVIDE FOOD AND SHELTER AND SECURITY FOR THEM.

MAYBE QUITTING MY JOB ON A WHIM WAS ABOUT THE DUMBEST THING I'VE EVER DONE.

I THINK YOU'RE WRONG.

ABOUT BEING A FOOL?

ABOUT ALL THE "MAYBES."

I CALLED FRED. HE THINKS PEMBROOK WILL BE RECEPTIVE TO MY WANTING TO COME BACK.

THAT'S GREAT.

APPARENTLY, I'VE REALLY BEEN MISSED.

I'M NOT SURPRISED.

ACCORDING TO FRED, OFFICE MORALE HASN'T BEEN THE SAME.

YOU'RE A SPECIAL PERSON, ROGER.

THE COMPUTERS HAVEN'T CRASHED IN THREE WEEKS!

SUSTAINED WORK! I CAN'T TAKE IT!

FOX, COME BAAACK!

WELL, WELL, IF IT ISN'T ROGER FOX DOWN ON BENDED KNEE, BEGGING FOR HIS JOB BACK.

MR. PEMBROOK, SIR, I—

AHEM.

MR. PEMBROOK, SIR, I—

IN CASE IT'S NOT OBVIOUS, I'VE MISSED YOU, FOX.

I SEE THE SHOE SHINE KIT IS IN ITS USUAL PLACE.

THE TRUTH OF THE MATTER, FOX, IS YOU'VE BEEN VERY HARD TO REPLACE.

APPARENTLY, IN TODAY'S JOB MARKET, PEOPLE WITH YOUR BUSINESS SKILLS MAKE SIX TIMES WHAT WE'VE BEEN PAYING YOU.

SO IF YOU'VE COME TO ASK FOR YOUR JOB BACK, THE ANSWER IS YES.

WITH NO CUT IN PAY?!

NOT THAT YOUR BUSINESS SKILLS ARE FLAWLESS.

OK, OK, A LITTLE CUT IN PAY.

YOU GOT YOUR JOB BACK?!

WAS THERE EVER ANY DOUBT?

HOORAY! YIPPEE! WOOHOO!

THERE'S JUST ONE CATCH, KIDS.

PEMBROOK'S COUNTING THESE LAST FEW WEEKS AS BURNED-UP VACATION TIME. WE'RE NOT GOING TO BE ABLE TO GO CAMPING THIS SUMMER AS WE'D PLANNED.

HOORAY! YIPPEE! WOOHOO!

THEY MUST HAVE MIS-HEARD ME. THEY'RE CHEERING LOUDER.

HOO-RAY! YIP-PEE! WOO-HOO!

FoxTrot

by Bill Amend

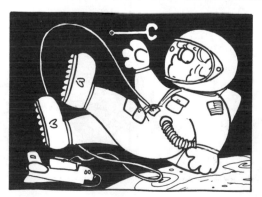

YOU HAVE NO IDEA HOW WEIRD IT IS TO FALL ASLEEP WITH YOU DRIVING.

WHAT WAS WITH THE TARZAN YELL?

SPLOTCH
SPLOTCH
SPLOTCH

SPLITCH
SPLOTCH
SPLOTCH

PAIGE, YOU LEFT THE SUNSCREEN ON THE KITCHEN COUNTER.

HUH? THEN WHAT'S THIS?

I HAVE GOT TO GET LIGHTER SUNGLASSES.

THAT'S ONE MUSTARD-YELLOW TAN YOU'VE GOT GOING.

WHAT'S THIS?

DAD MUST HAVE ACCIDENTALLY LEFT A HAMBURGER ON THE GRILL LAST NIGHT.

THAT MAN CAN DO THE MOST UNBELIEVABLE THINGS.

HERE, BIRDY-BIRDIES...

HEEEERE, BIRDY-BIRDIES...

FLY OVER HEEEEERE, BIRDY-BIRDIES...

WHAT I WOULDN'T GIVE TO BE DOCTOR DOLITTLE SOMETIMES.

GIVE IT UP.

GOTCHA!

HA! MISSED ME!

GOTCHA!

HA! MISSED AGAIN! I'M BEGINNING TO THINK I SHOULD BE WATERING OUR LAWN AT NIGHT. I THINK IT'S CUTE.

HEY!

I'VE NAMED THIS KITE THE SPF-10,000. I LIKE HOW YOU WROTE "HA HA" ON THE BOTTOM.

BACK WHEN I WAS FIVE, I COULDN'T CLIMB A TREE LIKE THIS AT ALL.

WHEN I WAS SEVEN, I COULD MAYBE GET ONTO THAT FIRST BRANCH.

BUT NOW THAT I'M 10, I CAN CLIMB ALL THE WAY TO THE VERY TOP WITH BARELY ANY EFFORT.

I KNEW I WAS TOO OLD TO SEE "TARZAN." YOUR MOM SAYS IF YOU CAN MOVE YOUR LEG, IT'S PROBABLY NOT BROKEN.

FoxTrot
by Bill Amend

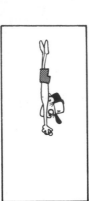

FORGET CHLORINE — POOLS WITH HIGH DIVES NEED TO PUT NOVOCAIN IN THE WATER.

TEN-PLUS, MR. LOUGANIS.

I SHOULD BE BACK IN A COUPLE HOURS.

WHERE ARE YOU GOING?

COMPUTER SHOPPING.

WAIT! WAIT! LET ME COME WITH YOU!

MAKE THAT SIX OR SEVEN HOURS.

WE'LL LEAVE A LIGHT ON.

ALL OF THESE COMPUTERS ARE SO MUCH MORE ADVANCED THAN OUR OLD ONE.

NO DUH.

HOT!

MOM, OUR OLD COMPUTER WAS ANCIENT! OBSOLETE! A FOSSILIZED RELIC FROM A BYGONE ERA! I CAN'T BELIEVE DAD FOUND A BUYER!

JASON, IT WAS THREE YEARS OLD.

EXACTLY.

HOT!

WELL, SPEAKING AS SOMEONE ABOUT TO TURN 43...

I'VE GOT NEWS FOR YOU, MOM...

HELLO. I'M THE OWNER OF THIS SUPER-STORE. HAVE YOU BEEN HELPED?

HOT!

PLEASE, MOM, PLEASE...GET THIS COMPUTER!

IT'S GOT DUAL PROCESSORS, TONS OF RAM, A STATE-OF-THE-ART 3-D CARD, A BUILT-IN DISK ARRAY, DVD, SLOTS GALORE, PORTS GALORE, AND DOLBY DIGITAL SURROUND SOUND OUTPUT!

IF YOU ASK ME, IT'S AWFULLY PLAIN.

PLAIN??

HAVE YOU SEEN THESE CUTE ONES IN ALL DIFFERENT COLORS OVER HERE?

"CUTE"? MOM, THIS IS CINDY CRAWFORD!

THIS IS THE COMPUTER YOU WANT?? AN iFRUIT??

IT'S SO DARLING.

I MEAN, LOOK AT WHAT IT SAYS WHEN YOU START IT UP.

"WELCOME TO iFRUIT. HUG ME."

OH, HUSH. I'VE SEEN YOU DO THIS.

iTHINK iWILL bSICK.

HELP ME OUT, JASON. I'M TORN.

OVER WHAT?

ACCORDING TO THAT SALESMAN OVER THERE, RUMOR HAS IT THAT THE iFRUIT LINE IS DUE FOR A MAJOR UPGRADE IN A FEW WEEKS.

SO DO I BUY ONE NOW, OR WAIT FOR THE SUPERIOR MODEL?

WHAT'LL IT HAVE? A FASTER PROCESSOR? MORE RAM? A BETTER 3-D CHIP?

A LAMBSKIN KEYBOARD.

YOU WANT TO SEE TORN? WATCH MY HAIR RIGHT NOW, MOTHER.

I GUESS THE ONLY QUESTION NOW IS WHICH FLAVOR OF iFRUIT TO GET.

GEEKDOM IS DEAD.

WE HAVE ALL 32 COLORS IN STOCK, BUT IF YOU WANT MANGO-KIWI, YOU SHOULD GET IT SOON. I HEAR THEY MAY DISCONTINUE THAT MODEL.

...AS IN RETIRE?

I WANT EVERY MANGO-KIWI YOU'VE GOT! DO YOU HEAR ME?! EVERY ONE!

SORRY, KID. I'M NOT ABOUT TO STOP HER.

THESE AREN'T BEANIE BABIES, MOM! COME BACK!

A TRUCK! A TRUCK! I NEED A TRUCK!

FoxTrot
by Bill Amend

THIS MANUAL BRAGS THAT THE iFRUIT CAN BE OUT OF THE BOX AND ON THE INTERNET IN AS LITTLE AS 10 MINUTES.

THAT HAS TO BE A TYPO.

IT *IS* HARD TO BELIEVE.

WE SET UP THAT LINUX SERVER AT CAMP IN, WHAT, 30 SECONDS?

ONLY BECAUSE YOU TANGLED THE CABLES, MR. SLOWPOKE.

WELCOME TO iFRUIT.

WOULD YOU LIKE HELP CONFIGURING YOUR DESKTOP? NO.

WOULD YOU LIKE HELP CONNECTING TO THE INTERNET? NO.

WOULD YOU LIKE TO RUN MY HELPFUL ONLINE TUTORIAL?

NO! NO! NO! I WANT TO FIGURE YOU OUT THE HARD WAY!

I COULD RUN MY TUTORIAL WITH THE SOUND OFF.

I SAID NO TUTORIAL!

BONK!

BONK!

BONK! BONK! BONK!

I ASSUME *EVENTUALLY* YOU'LL TELL DAD IT HAS NO FLOPPY DRIVE.

EVENTUALLY.

BONK! BONK! BONK! BONK! BONK! BONK! BONK! BONK! BONK! BONK!

DARE I ASK? — **THAT OUTFIT CLASHED WITH THE iFRUIT.**

JASON, WOULD YOU MIND INSTALLING THIS EXTRA RAM INTO THE iFRUIT?

WOW. THIS LOOKS REALLY COMPLICATED. YOU PRACTICALLY HAVE TO TAKE THE WHOLE COMPUTER APART.

I CAN'T BELIEVE HOW MANY PAIN-IN-THE-NECK STEPS THERE ARE.

I THOUGHT THAT WOULD PUT A SMILE ON YOUR FACE. — **YOU KNOW, MAYBE I CAN LIKE THIS THING.**

SO WHAT'S THE VERDICT ON MOM'S NEW COMPUTER? — **IT'S GROWING ON ME.**

YOU KNOW HOW WITH OUR OLD COMPUTER MOM WOULD NEVER BUY COOL THINGS LIKE SCANNERS AND DIGITIZING TABLETS BECAUSE THEY WERE TOO EXPENSIVE?

WELL, THE iFRUIT SOLVES THAT PROBLEM IN A BIG WAY.

iFRUIT PERIPHERALS ARE AFFORDABLE? — **CLOSE.** — **BANANA-ORANGE CD-ROM BURNERS! AREN'T THEY ADORABLE?!**

FoxTrot
by Bill Amend

WHAT'S WITH THE VIDEO CAMERA?

WE'RE SHOOTING A MOVIE.

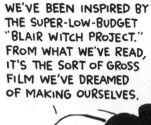

WE'VE BEEN INSPIRED BY THE SUPER-LOW-BUDGET "BLAIR WITCH PROJECT." FROM WHAT WE'VE READ, IT'S THE SORT OF GROSS FILM WE'VE DREAMED OF MAKING OURSELVES.

I SAW IT LAST WEEK. IT WASN'T THAT GORY.

I MEANT GROSS IN THE $100 MILLION SENSE.

I'D ROLL MY EYES, BUT THOSE MUSCLES ARE TIRED.

"DAY ONE: NO SIGN OF THE PAIGE WITCH. PERHAPS SHE *IS* JUST A MYTH."...

SHE MIGHT BE AT THE MALL.

In 1999, two students went on a search for the fabled Paige Witch.

They were never heard from again.

This video tape is all that remains.

TRUST ME. SHE'LL DESTROY IT, TOO.

WE HAVE A STRATEGY.

WE'RE RECORDING ON THE TAPE WITH HER EIGHTH-GRADE GRADUATION.

This video tape is all

HERE'S A LOCAL. LET'S TALK TO HIM.

EXCUSE ME, SIR, I'D LIKE TO ASK YOU A FEW QUESTIONS ABOUT THE PAIGE WITCH.

FIRST, WAS SHE ALWAYS UGLY?

DAD, YOU **CAN'T** BE LATE FOR WORK — IT'S SATURDAY!

SOME WEIRD THINGS ARE DEFINITELY AFOOT.

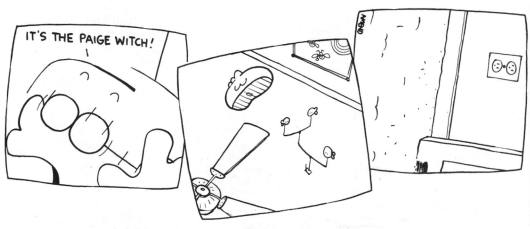

120

FoxTrot
by Bill Amend

FoxTrot

by Bill Amend

Panel 1:

HEY, ABBY — LOOKIN' GOOD.

MY NAME'S NOT ABBY, STEVE.

Panel 2:

ADELLE?... ADRIENNE?... AGATHA?... ALEXIS?... ALLISON?... AMANDA?... ANASTASIA?... ANGELICA?... ANN?... ANNA?... ANNE?... ASHLEY?... AUDREY?... BARBARA?... BECKY?... BETH?... BETHANY?...

WEIRDO.

Panel 3:

I DIDN'T WANT TO ASK WHY YOU HAD A "BABY NAMES" BOOK IN YOUR BACKPACK.

SUMMER VACATION WREAKS HAVOC WITH MY MEMORY.

Panel 4:

YOUR TEACHER CALLED TODAY, JASON.

OH?

Panel 5:

SHE SAYS YOU'VE BEEN HIDING MAGAZINES IN YOUR TEXTBOOKS AND READING THEM DURING CLASS HOURS.

Panel 6:

SHE SAYS SHE DOESN'T KNOW WHAT TO DO WITH YOU.

Panel 7:

ONE IDEA WAS TO LET YOU GUEST-LECTURE.

THE AMERICAN JOURNAL OF PHYSICS ISN'T REALLY A "MAGAZINE," BY THE WAY.

Panel 8:

OK, CLASS, THIS WEEKEND I WANT YOU TO DO CHAPTER ONE, PROBLEMS 8-12, 15, 17, 19, 24, 25, 30-40 AND 42.

Panel 9:

PETER, YOU HAVE A QUESTION?

COULDN'T YOU JUST E-MAIL US THIS, SO WE DON'T HAVE TO BOTHER WRITING IT ALL DOWN?

Panel 10:

WHAT WAS THAT, SIR?

Panel 11:

WELL, HE CERTAINLY SIMPLIFIED THINGS FOR YOU, MR. E-MAIL.

HOW AM I SUPPOSED TO DO **EVERY** PROBLEM IN THE BOOK?!

FoxTrot
by Bill Amend

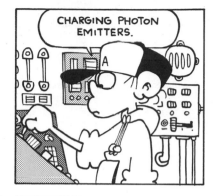

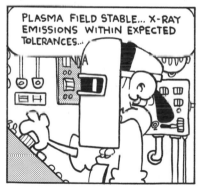